NEXT STOP: *The Afterlife*

"C. S. Lewis once said, 'If you read history you will find that the Christians who did most for the present world were just those who thought most of the next.' Lewis's *The Great Divorce* is an incredible journey into the afterlife, and Dr. Swafford is the perfect person in this present world to be your guide. Don't miss this opportunity to live the truths of the next life in your life today."

Kevin Cotter
Head of studios at Hallow

"*The Great Divorce* is such a beautiful and theologically rich book, and it is a delight to have Andrew Swafford walk us through all of its nuances. Swafford not only gives us deeper insights into the meaning of this impactful story but also offers wisdom on how these lessons of virtue can be lived out in our daily lives as Catholics!"

Jackie Angel
Catholic speaker and author of *Memorize Scripture*

"C. S. Lewis's *The Great Divorce* is so rich and profound that one hesitates to recommend any book about it, given that rereading *The Great Divorce* itself is generally far better. But Andrew Swafford has done the seemingly impossible. By describing the conversations that structure *The Great Divorce* and then delivering his own insights, in dialogue with other thinkers such as Tolkien and Karol Wojtyła, Swafford calls us to the life of ego-renouncing virtue and invites us to say yes to God and heavenly life in the present moment, in the midst of the sufferings that tempt us toward vice and self-destruction. A marvelous spiritual guidebook!"

Matthew Levering
James N. Jr. and Mary D. Perry Chair of Theology at
Mundelein Seminary at the University of St. Mary of the Lake

"Faith and love are the subjects of many sermons and books. Hope, on the other hand, is glossed over. No one talks about it. At last, a book appears that will stand in the breach and discuss heaven in a way that will make everybody excited to go there. In *Next Stop: The Afterlife*, Andrew Swafford, with the help of C. S. Lewis, shows us how the earthly pleasures we are so often attached to are no more than faint glimmers of the glory, beauty, and joy to come. All preachers, teachers, and, indeed, all Christians must read this book."

Marcellino D'Ambrosio
Catholic author and international speaker

"I consider Dr. Andrew Swafford to be many things: a trusted friend, a virtuous husband and father, and a remarkable theologian. After reading *Next Stop: The Afterlife*, I have added 'master catechist' to that list. Unpacking *The Great Divorce,* one of the most underrated books (in my opinion) of the twentieth century, is no small task; but Swafford has done a masterful job of taking complex theological realities and—like C. S. Lewis himself—making them profoundly simple. This book is a gift, a road map, and a companion to help guide us not just through a great Christian classic but straight to heaven. Filled with practical wisdom, invaluable insights, and humble reminders, this book serves as an arrow pointing our moral compasses directly back to the arms of our Heavenly Father."

Mark Hart
Chief innovation officer at Life Teen International

NEXT STOP: *The Afterlife*

Unveiling the Truth of Heaven and Hell with C. S. Lewis's *The Great Divorce*

Andrew Swafford

Ave Maria Press AVE Notre Dame, Indiana

Founded in 1865, Ave Maria Press is a ministry of the United States Province of Holy Cross.

www.avemariapress.com

Paperback: ISBN-13 978-1-64680-409-2

E-book: ISBN-13 978-1-64680-410-8

Cover images © Theodor Vasile and Abhishek Shintre from Unsplash.

Cover and text design by Andy Wagoner.

Printed and bound in the United States of America.

Library of Congress Cataloging-in-Publication Data is available.

Contents

Introduction

C. S. Lewis wrote *The Great Divorce* just after World War II, around the time he published *Mere Christianity* and *The Screwtape Letters. The Great Divorce* describes the split between heaven and hell, the irreconcilable chasm between the two. It begins with a fictional bus ride, where people who have died get off in the afterlife. They, in effect, have a choice to stay in the "grey town" or journey to the mountain country (which is symbolic of heaven). As they journey to the mountain country, they are met by various people, often people they knew earlier in life. Usually, there is some lingering issue that needs to be addressed before they can progress into the mountain country, some sin or attachment for which they must take responsibility and from which they must turn. For many characters, this issue proves insurmountable, leading them to halt their progress or turn back altogether toward the grey town.

Those coming from the grey town are called "ghosts," and those from the mountain country are typically referred to as "bright spirits" (sometimes capitalized as "Spirit"). As we will see, those in the grey town are less real, less substantial than those in the mountain country—and less real than the bright spirits who reside in the mountain country. Indeed, this is the heart of the book: Those who continue the journey into the mountain country become *like* the mountain country. They are transformed and become radiant and more fully real than they were in the grey town, and far more real than they ever were in their earthly lives.

I have used *The Great Divorce* for many years in my Christian Moral Life class at Benedictine College (along with other books by C. S. Lewis), where I have taught philosophy and theology since 2007. In fact, *The Great Divorce* has become my favorite book about heaven. Even though we ought to long for heaven as the ultimate aspiration of our lives, I have found that many of us (including myself on occasion) have trouble doing so. We subconsciously find it difficult to imagine heaven as enjoyable—just idly sitting around "forever," praising God for all eternity. Even though we know with our minds that heaven is the human heart's deepest longing, we often do not feel this truth viscerally within our hearts. *The Great Divorce* dramatically addresses our dilemma. It powerfully brings out the way in which "no eye has seen, nor ear heard . . . what God has prepared for those who love him" (1 Cor 2:9). As we will see, heaven is all that is fully real. Everything else is only a shadowy imitation by comparison.

What emerges in Lewis's work is a truly typological (and sacramental) view of reality. Just as the persons, events, and institutions of the Old Testament (e.g., Eve, Isaac, Passover, manna, the ark of the covenant, Moses, David, the Temple) prefigure greater realities to come in the New (e.g., Mary, Jesus, the Eucharist, and so on; see *Catechism of the Catholic Church* [*CCC*], 128–129), so also our experiences of this life point beyond themselves to heaven itself. What we cherish the most in this life—our encounters with the true, good, and beautiful; our experiences of joy, communion, and intimacy—foreshadows something even greater to come. This earthly life is truly good; but it is the appetizer, the hors d'oeuvre, for what lies beyond.

So, if we ever wonder if we'll be bored in heaven, we should look first to the earthly foreshadowing immediately present before us. Do we love and cherish the very best things in this life, the moments that most closely approximate pure joy, intimacy, and communion—the times we feel noticed, understood, and cared for, truly seen and known? Those moments are signs pointing beyond themselves to the perfect joy, intimacy, and communion we will experience in the next life. This is what *The Great Divorce* brings out so splendidly, and it is the patrimony of Catholic and Christian faith. Consider C. S. Lewis's words in *Mere Christianity* regarding the goodness of this life and how it points beyond itself to the next:

> If I find in myself a desire which no experience in this world can satisfy, the most probable explanation is that I was made for another world. If none of my earthly pleasures satisfy it, that does not prove that the universe is a fraud. Probably earthly pleasures were never meant to satisfy it, but only to arouse it, to suggest the real thing. If that is so, I must take care, on the one hand, never to despise, or be unthankful for, these earthly blessings, and on the other, never to mistake them for the something else of which they are only a kind of copy, or echo, or mirage. I must keep alive in myself the desire for my true country, which I shall not find till after death; I must never let it get snowed under or turned aside; I must make it the main object of life to press on to that other country and to help others to do the same.[1]

After St. Augustine's conversion back to the Catholic faith, he recounts a conversation he had with his mother, Monica, shortly before her death. They both seem to intuit the nearness of her passing, as they discuss what heaven will be like.[2] Their reflection moves in the same sacramental and typological manner described above, from creatures to the Uncreated God: "We lifted ourselves in longing yet more ardent toward *That Which Is*, and step by step traversed all bodily creatures."[3] As the book of Wisdom teaches, "From the greatness and beauty of created things comes a corresponding perception of their Creator" (13:5).

"Everything that exists is good," says St. Augustine, and all things are ontologically "true insofar as they exist."[4] Insofar as a thing exists, then, it is true, good, and beautiful.[5] Every finite thing participates in the gift of existence; but the fullness of existence is found in God himself, the ground of all being. "Contemplating other things below you [God]," Augustine writes, "I saw that they do not in the fullest sense exist, nor yet are they completely non-beings: they are real because they are from you, but unreal inasmuch as they are not what you are."[6] In other words, everything we see participates—in its own finite way—in truth, goodness, and beauty, the infinite perfections of which are found in God himself.

We human beings are thirsting for the real, thirsting for truth, goodness, and beauty—yearning for communion and happiness. This thirst is at root a longing for God and for heaven. As we journey through life and as we grow in virtue, we become more like God. In this sense, we become more real, more fit for our heavenly end. This is what *The Great Divorce* is all about. In this fictional account, we come face-to-face with ourselves, face-to-face with the dramatic choice of our lives—either to embrace the fullness of joy and the fullness of the real, or to prefer the abyss of nothingness, isolation, and despair. This choice ultimately brooks no middle ground. This is the "great divorce." In the end, it is either God or nothing, and it's a choice we are constantly making in the present moment.

My hope in this work is that we come away with greater clarity and conviction regarding our own story and where we are going. Life is too short to simply float by. The insights of Lewis's *The Great Divorce* empower us to live with greater intentionality and purpose, with heaven as the true goal of our lives and the ultimate fulfillment of every human desire.

I do not presume that everyone reading this book has already read *The Great Divorce*, nor is there a need to have a copy close at hand. The goal here is to share the fruits of his work and its application to our lives today, something my students have cherished for many years. By recourse to these fictional characters in Lewis's work, we catch important glimpses of the reality of heaven and the ultimate truth of our lives. Our task is to live with heaven in mind and to see everything else in that light. As we learn to do so, nothing else will ever be the same.

Chapters 1–7 concern characters in *The Great Divorce* and their spiritual struggles (e.g., with faith, anger, forgiveness, humility, lust). Chapter 8 brings out the heart of Lewis's work hinted at above—that heaven is more fully *real* than hell, and far more real than this earthly life. Chapter 9 draws from the end of *The Great Divorce*, where Lewis discusses the mysterious interrelation between time and eternity, how God's vision of things outside of time relates to our experience of living out the drama of our lives *within* time.

As we turn to chapters 10 and 11, we seek to apply what we have gained from Lewis to our own lives and the dramatic choice before us. Here, we draw from thinkers such as St. John Paul II and St. Augustine to illumine our path, discussing the *two ways*—the way of death and the way of life (chapter 10)—and our preparation for the coming of the Bridegroom, Christ Jesus (chapter 11), at the end of time and especially at the hour of our death. Being ready in the present for Christ's coming makes all the difference.

ONE

Are There Really Intellectual *Sins?*

In the modern context, we typically do not think of intellectual sins (or intellectual virtues). For instance, we might describe someone as "virtuous and wise," considering wisdom as something added to virtue but not necessarily a part of it. But for classical thinkers such as Aristotle, there is a significant place for *intellectual* virtues, as the perfections of the intellectual powers latent within our human nature.[1] If we have powers of intellect, will, and emotions/passions, then leaving any of these powers dormant or unfulfilled leads to unhappiness. Conversely, fulfilling these powers by fully actualizing them in accordance with our human nature is what virtue and happiness are all about.[2] Virtue enables us to become *more*, while vice turns us inward, making us a lesser version of ourselves.

In today's world, we generally don't consider intellectual virtues or intellectual sins because we have radically divorced the head and the heart, truth and love, "right brain" and "left brain," as it were. Still, we maintain some place for bad intellectual habits, such as prejudice and dishonesty, retaining an awareness of the connection between intellect and will, particularly the way in which the will can hinder our ability to see and grasp the truth.

This is what is at issue with the "Episcopal Ghost" of *The Great Divorce*.[3] He had been a bishop earlier in life (presumably Anglican) and had pushed the envelope of intellectual speculation regarding the faith well beyond the bounds of Christian orthodoxy. "Dick," his friend earlier in life (and now a bright spirit from the mountain country), explains to the bishop that the bishop was in the grey town for being an "apostate."[4] The bishop had spiritualized the faith away, to the point of denying any concrete reality to things like heaven, hell, or even the Resurrection of Jesus, thus vacating the faith of its objective content.[5]

The sticking point in their dialogue, however, is not so much the bishop's conclusions, as it is *why* he came to them.

Dick asks the bishop directly, "Do you really think there are no sins of intellect?" The bishop responds emphatically that such sins exist, pointing to prejudice, dishonesty, timidity, and stagnation. But then he insists, "*Honest opinions* fearlessly followed—they are not sins."[6]

Earlier in their conversation, the bishop made known how he thought Dick had become "rather narrow-minded" toward the end of his life, because Dick had begun to take seriously the literal reality of heaven and hell. With deep irony, Dick responds, "*But wasn't I right?*" The bishop continues his standard line of thinking, suggesting that of course such things could be true in a "*spiritual sense*," but beyond that they are nothing but superstition and mythology. The bishop is apparently unaware of what the grey town truly is and the gravity of the choice before him.[7]

Honest Opinions

Everything turns on the phrase "honest opinions," which becomes the hinge point of their dialogue. The bishop pleads with Dick, stating that he made himself vulnerable, risking everything, even to the point of courageously rejecting the core of the Christian faith: "When the doctrine of the Resurrection ceased to commend itself to the critical faculties which God had given me, I openly rejected it. I preached my famous sermon. . . . I took every risk."[8]

Dick responds by noting that the bishop's supposed "risk" brought nothing but "popularity, sales . . . and finally a bishopric." He goes on to challenge the conceptions he and the bishop each had earlier in life, explaining how they were really afraid of a "breach with the spirit of the age." They figured out very quickly in college what kinds of viewpoints got good grades and won approval, to the point where Dick asks poignantly, "*When did we put up one moment's real resistance to the loss of our faith?*"[9]

The bishop is disgusted, suggesting that Dick is simply disparaging liberal theology; but Dick insists that this is not about generalities—it is only about the two of them, the real issue being their fear of ridicule and not fitting in.

The Heart as Key to the Head

As both Dick and the bishop allowed themselves to be carried along by the intellectual current of the age, they eventually came to believe the viewpoints they were entertaining. As Lewis put it in another work, "All mortals tend to turn into the thing they are pretending to be."[10]

We easily do the same today—perhaps at work or with neighbors or acquaintances. We all want to fit in. "There is a subtle play of looks and tones and laughs," writes Lewis, "by which a mortal can imply he is of the same party as those to whom he is speaking."[11] Even if our initial motivation is to fit in, with time we tend to embrace the views we surround ourselves with. These habits of mind become part of our ingrained disposition and mental makeup. What began as a desire for acceptance became full-throttled skepticism for both Dick and the bishop. As Dick explains, "Having allowed oneself to drift, unresisting, unpraying, accepting half-conscious solicitation from our desires, we reached a point where we no longer believed the Faith. Just in the same way, a jealous man, drifting and unresisting, reaches a point at which he believes lies about his best friend."[12]

In this sense, Lewis suggests we are indeed culpable for our intellectual errors—not so much because we took a misstep in our theology, but because of the motivation that led us there, often having more to do with moral weakness than a sincere pursuit of truth.

Dick begs the bishop to repent: "You have seen Hell [the grey town]; you are in sight of Heaven. Will you, even now, repent and believe?" He continues, "Will you come with me to the mountains? It will hurt at first, until your feet are hardened. Reality is harsh to the feet of shadows. But will you come?"[13]

The bishop hesitates, asking for "some assurances," particularly about his *usefulness* in heaven. Dick declines to respond. Clearly the bishop's desire to be useful and important is a vestige of his attachment to his own ego, his sense of self-importance. All of us deeply desire to be seen, known, and loved. But the chasm the bishop must cross is letting go of himself, letting go of how seriously he takes himself. The challenge for the bishop is to have the humility to come to "the land not of questions but of answers."[14]

This is precisely what the bishop cannot handle—not earlier in life and not now. He resists the very idea of his intellect coming to rest, because he would rather play "intellectual ping-pong," always entertaining an infinite array of opinions with perpetual openness. As he asserts, "Ah, but we must interpret those beautiful words in our own way! For me there is no such thing as a final answer. The free wind of inquiry must *always* continue to blow through the mind, must it not? 'Prove all things' . . . to travel hopefully is better than to arrive."[15]

Trenchantly, Dick points out, "If that were true . . . how could anyone travel *hopefully*? There would be nothing to hope for." A child asks questions with the hope of finding answers. An open mind is good for the purpose of latching on to the truth when it becomes apparent—the goal is *knowing*, not permanent seeking. The bishop's problem is that his intellectual inquiry has more to do with his own self-aggrandizement than a sincere desire for answers. It has become about him, rather than a genuine quest for truth. "Once you knew what inquiry was for," Dick exhorts. "There was a time when you asked questions because you wanted answers and were glad you had found them. Become that child again: even now."[16]

Truth and Values

The bishop had fallen into believing that there is an unbridgeable chasm between matters of fact and religious (or moral) values, a fact-value split very common in our modern context.[17] Only matters of fact are said to be "true" or "false" because only matters of fact can be quantified and measured. Therefore, truth is present *only* in the scientific world, accessible solely through the scientific method. Consequently, everything that does not fit within the scientific method—that which can't be seen, touched, or measured or can't fit in a test tube—is relegated to the subjective realm of values. Ethics and religion fall into this latter category, with the result that one can never come to truth in this area. Accordingly, when it comes to morality or religion, all we can do is subjectively assert what we value—we cannot get beyond complete and indifferent relativism.

How many people subconsciously assume this point of view—that there is no such thing as *truth* in religion or in philosophical questions regarding God, the human person, or morality? To use Pope Benedict XVI's memorable phrase, we find ourselves living under the "dictatorship of relativism."[18]

When the pro-life position, for example, is disparaged as merely an attempt to impose one's religious faith upon others, we can see this mentality at work. It is as if reason has no capacity to discuss morality, as if there are no moral facts of the matter. Most people do not really believe this, but many still pay lip service to it, as if this view were entailed by our scientific age.[19] The result is that we relegate that which is most human—religion and the moral life—to the subjective and unknowable, somehow deeming them insignificant and not central to human life.[20]

Dick puts the heavenly truth directly before the bishop: "We know nothing of speculation [here in the mountain country]. Come and see. I will bring you to Eternal Fact, the Father of all other facthood." The bishop's strongly ingrained habits of mind cause him to balk: "I should object very strongly to describing God as a 'fact.' The Supreme Value would surely be a less inadequate description."[21]

The conversation ends abruptly as the bishop remembers he has a paper to present in the grey town for a *theological* society there (ironically enough!). The bishop's yearning to be needed and praised is stronger than his desire to rest in the eternal truth of God; his desire for self-importance wins out over his feigned humility as an intellectual seeker. The bishop explains a bit about his paper: Since Jesus died relatively young, he likely would have outgrown his earlier views, if only he had lived longer. "I am going to ask my audience to consider what his mature views would have been. . . . What a different Christianity we might have had if only the Founder had reached his full stature!"[22]

Here is the perennial temptation to turn Jesus into whatever we want him to be, the temptation to prefer an à la carte faith, custom designed to our tastes—and custom made to fit with the spirit of the age in which we live.

Like the bishop, each of the characters we will meet in the following chapters has a choice, a choice that parallels their choices earlier in life. The grey town also begins to emerge with greater clarity. It is both hell *and* purgatory: hell for those who remain and purgatory for those who progress toward the mountain country.

In the next chapter, we apply some of the lessons learned from the bishop's story as we look more deeply at the nature of faith and intellectual courage, attempting to forge a path amid the intellectual currents flowing rapidly against us today.

TWO

Faith and the Heart

The story of the bishop shows us that there is far more at work than dispassionate intellectual inquiry when it comes to profound religious and philosophical questions. Especially when we are concerned with questions about God and morality, we are deeply invested in these answers, as we are putting ourselves out there with every position we take. Here, there is no neutrality, no disinterested discussion—no truly "naked" public square. To act and speak as if God is irrelevant to human life *is* to take a position on God and his importance (or the lack thereof). This is the mistake of secular liberalism: to assume that secularism is not a worldview—that it, itself, is not a fundamental claim about reality, about what truly matters. In this sense, everyone has a "theology." Everyone has a position on what matters most, even if never fully articulated. To act as if economics, politics, technology, and the maintenance of our youthful appearance at all costs are the highest values *is* to take a position on God (and his irrelevance).

We are all influenced by the various cultures around us, by our friends, family, the media, and so forth. The challenge of modern life, as with the bishop above, is that God and the supernatural all too often fade from our horizon—not so much rejected as *ignored*. We want to fit in and not look *too* radical. As God and the things of God fade from our vantage point, he becomes less and less real in our minds and hearts. We come to live in a disenchanted universe, as we are no longer able to perceive the sacred around us. Eventually, we become numb to the effect of this dynamic upon us. This is no mere intellectual conclusion but very much a moral and spiritual one as well.

Intellectual Courage

Philosopher and legal scholar Robert George once described an exercise he undertook with his students at Princeton University. He asked who among them would have been abolitionists in the 1830s, had they lived in the southern portion of the United States at that time. Of course, all his students unanimously and enthusiastically raised their hands. George told them that he would accept their claim if they could provide examples of standing up for the marginalized *at great personal cost to themselves*, resulting in their becoming unpopular with peers, entailing their loss of gainful employment and graduate school opportunities, and leading to their being despised and scorned by the powerful.[1]

His point hits home. It is easy *now* to say that we would have been abolitionists then—because it costs us virtually nothing to say this today. In fact, it would be far more costly to say otherwise, since to stand against racism today (as we, no doubt, should) curries favor with the powerful. But to stand up for the unborn and for marriage between one man and one woman, to challenge the commodification of human life through in vitro fertilization and other reproductive technologies, or to question the morality of assisted suicide is to go against the grain of the elite today. In Pope Francis's words, the "throwaway culture" of today has no place for the unborn, the handicapped, and the elderly because they are no longer "useful" to us.[2]

As with the bishop (and Dick earlier in life), there is constant danger of melding our views to fit with our time. This is true of every generation. What has intellectual currency and cachet changes with the vagaries of time and place. Do we have the *courage* to stand on conviction, or will we simply bend to the spirit of the age? In the words of St. Paul, there is "one faith, one Lord, one baptism . . . so that we may no longer be children, tossed back and forth and carried about with every wind of doctrine" (Eph 4:5, 14). For a Catholic, this is why the living magisterium is so important, a teaching authority that speaks with the authority of Christ.[3]

Each age has aspects of divine revelation that are more difficult to accept than others (and aspects of divine revelation that fit more seamlessly with one's own time than others). For example, the teaching of Matthew 25 on the corporal works of mercy—that we will be judged based on how we treat the least among us—fits well with the contemporary emphasis on social justice. But Jesus's teaching on the seriousness of lust and the need for sexual purity and sexual integration does not fit so well with the mentality of modern man (see Matthew 5:27–28 and 1 Corinthians 6:9–10)—nor does his insistence on the reality of hell (see Matthew 5:29–30, 25:41; *CCC* 1033–37). Christians in every age are called to be a sign of contradiction, to hold to the fullness of the Gospel of Jesus Christ, even at the price of not fitting in with the regnant ethos of the day. An à la carte approach to the faith is by definition always a dilution of the faith.[4]

It would be a strange thing, frankly, if everything God revealed matched perfectly with what we already thought. Such a scenario should give us pause. If that were the case, we might suspect we were dealing with a purely man-made religion, one suited to our likings. God's revealed truth *should* challenge us; it should make us feel uncomfortable at points—that is actually a sign of its authenticity as the Word of God. After all, if we simply made it up, we would surely have it agree with our sympathies and passions. The fact that Christianity pushes against the grain of so many of our impulses is a perennial sign of its supernatural truth.[5]

Given that secularism is not letting up any time soon, if our faith is important to us, we must *feed* it. As Lewis once asked rhetorically, is it not the case that most people who lose their faith simply "drift"?[6] Typically, people drift from the faith because they get caught up in the spirit of the age and gradually lose their spiritual moorings. This is often accompanied by a slackening in spiritual practices (such as prayer and the sacraments) and a weakening of bonds to the Christian community. As years go by, some people find themselves no longer "believing" the faith—sometimes not realizing exactly how they got there.

We turn next to look at the nature of faith and how we can nurture the gift of faith, in hopes of sustaining our earthly pilgrimage to the Father's house.

Two Aspects of Faith

Faith has two aspects, two dimensions, as it were—one intellectual and the other a matter of personal entrustment to the living God. On the one hand, faith perfects and elevates the intellect. It teaches us *truths* we could never know otherwise, truths about who God is and what he has done for us (such as the Trinity, the Incarnation, the Holy Eucharist, and the life of grace, which makes us sons and daughters of the Father in Christ and through the Spirit).

A powerful image that captures this intellectual aspect of faith is looking up at the stars at night. Faith is like seeing at night, whereas reason is like seeing during the day. We can see far deeper into outer space at night, but it's not as clear. During the day, we can see more clearly but not as deeply into the cosmos. Even though faith always entails some darkness (hence, the image of seeing at night), it remains a way of *knowing*, a way of seeing the truth of reality with more piercing insight and depth than reason could ever muster on its own.

On the other hand, faith is about more than just intellectual assent—it is also a matter of personal trust. After all, the demons see and "believe" in one sense (see James 2:19). An image that captures faith as personal trust is that of a tightrope walker. Imagine a tightrope walker asking a crowd, "Do you *believe* I can walk across this tightrope?" As the crowd responds with enthusiasm, the tightrope walker crosses the tightrope and the crowd cheers. Now imagine that the tightrope walker asks the crowd if they believe he can cross the tightrope while pushing a wheelbarrow. As the crowd cheers, he completes the task again, pushing a wheelbarrow across the tightrope. And now imagine him asking the crowd, "Do you believe I can push the wheelbarrow across the tightrope, *with somebody in the wheelbarrow*?" As the crowd cheers, eager to see if this feat is possible, he asks, "*Who's ready to get in?*"

To give a similar illustration, imagine ice skating on a frozen lake. It is one thing to *believe* (intellectually) that the lake is frozen while remaining on the sidelines. It is another thing altogether to get out there and *skate*.[7] That's what saving faith is all about, personally entrusting our lives to the living God—far more than mere "belief."

The Greek and Hebrew words for faith (*pistis* and *emunah*, respectively) mean something more like *faithfulness* or *allegiance*. Biblical and Christian faith takes a stand upon the living God and his truth (see Isaiah 7:9).[8] It makes a personal *commitment*, where we entrust ourselves to Jesus as Lord of our entire life. Here, we take the *risk* of faith.[9]

The bishop in the previous chapter lacks true faith in both ways. He came to believe that the Christian faith did not reveal *truths* but only concerned subjective values, gutting the Christian faith of any claim to objective reality (and so he lacks faith in the intellectual sense). This lack of true conviction made it impossible for him to entrust himself fully to the living God. If "God" is no more than an idea—a "supreme value"—one cannot give their life over to him in a personal, living, and fully committed way. Thus, the bishop could not take the risk of faith.

Heart and Head in Unison

The journey of faith is dynamic and lifelong. As with any relationship, there is an interactive combination of intellect, will, and emotional or affective bond that links us to another. For example, in the context of friendship:

- What do we *believe* about this particular person? What do we believe they stand for? (intellect)
- What is our *disposition* toward them? Where do they rank among our priorities and commitments? (will)
- What is our *affective* warmth toward them? Is our heart attuned to theirs? (emotional/affective bond)

Very often, the surest anchor for faith is from the bottom up. In other words, if the affective and emotional connection is present, the will and intellect are likely to follow. That is why marketing is so effective—it stirs our passions to persuade our intellect (and thereby move our will) to purchase things we do not necessarily need.[10]

For this reason, our affective connection (to God and others) is vitally important, but we cannot stop there. We cannot sustain the journey of faith with a Christian heart and a secular head—that is, we cannot sustain faith without serious intellectual conviction and commitment. In my experience, the most powerful way to foster faith is to sandwich the top and bottom aspects above—our affective connection to the Lord *and* our intellectual conviction, because the commitment of the will is likely to follow when both are present.[11]

Intellectual formation alone will not stave off the power of sin (nor the subtle influences to which the bishop succumbed). Neither can emotional enthusiasm alone sustain the journey of faith, since emotion is transitory by nature. We need to form ourselves and nurture our faith in all three areas: intellectually (by fostering our conviction in the truth of the faith); in the commitment of our will (by making God the highest priority of our lives, not merely in word but also in deed); and in our affective/emotional attachment and attunement to God (by allowing the truth of the faith to inform and influence our emotional lives—enabling us to *feel* the truth of the faith viscerally, attaching us all the more firmly to the faith).[12] If our faith matters to us, we must feed it. Otherwise, any one of us could end up like the bishop. May we never be so naïve as to think such a fate could never befall us.

We may not think of intellectual sins in the way people did when heresy was a capital crime across Europe in Catholic and Protestant countries alike.[13] But we can become negligent, and even culpable, in our loss of faith (see *CCC* 2123–2128).[14] If we tend to our intellectual formation in the faith (intellect) *and* foster a life of prayer and devotion and friendships rooted in the faith (affective), this is the surest path to faithfully loving the Lord Jesus to the very end (with the firm and enduring commitment of our will). Of course, faith is also a gift for which we must never cease to pray. In fact, prayer is essential to growth in faith, and so we turn now to a deeper discussion of prayer and its central role in the Christian journey.

The Importance of Prayer

Prayer is crucial for fostering this threefold dimension of our relationship with God (intellect, will, and emotion). It is vital for growing in both aspects of faith, the intellectual aspect and our personal entrustment to the Lord.[15] Prayer and faith go hand in hand. Sometimes we let prayer go because we are busy and "don't have time" (*CCC* 2726). Too often, we simply (and unwittingly) accept the mindset of the present age, which has no place for God and no real use for prayer, as the *Catechism* comments here:

> Certain attitudes deriving from the *mentality* of this "present world" can penetrate our lives if we are not vigilant. For example, some would have it that only that is true which can be verified by reason and science; yet prayer is a mystery that overflows both our conscious and unconscious lives.

> Others overly prize production and profit; thus, prayer being unproductive, is useless. . . . Some see prayer as a flight from the world in reaction against activism; but in fact, Christian prayer is neither an escape from reality nor a divorce from life. (2727, emphasis in original)

The "most common yet most hidden temptation" that keeps us from prayer is "*our lack of faith*" (*CCC* 2732, emphasis in original). No doubt, this is true in the bishop's story and others like it. Prayer, itself, is an act of faith—which thereby grows our faith. Conversely, opting not to pray, as the *Catechism* points out here, is a subtle expression of unbelief—which, over time, causes our faith to erode and wither.

We must ask ourselves, what are we making time *for*? What are we prioritizing? Our time and our priorities indicate where our hearts truly lie. We cannot claim to pray unceasingly if we do not set aside some "specific times" for prayer (see *CCC* 2697), just as we cannot claim to love all humanity if we do not intentionally love the people within our circle.

Prayer keeps us on track; it keeps us focused and curbs us when we wander. Consistent prayer is a self-corrective against merely following our appetite and the aggrandizement of our egos. This is so significant to our journey. Almost every instance of someone losing their faith will at some point include their falling away from consistent and heartfelt prayer, so much so that the *Catechism*'s citation here of St. Alphonsus Liguori is ominous but realistic: "Those who pray are certainly saved; those who do not pray are certainly damned" (cited in 2744).[16]

Our relationship with God is never static. Like a garden, it needs tending. In the words of Karol Wojtyła (later St. John Paul II), "Love is never something ready-made. . . . Love in a sense never 'is,' but only constantly 'becomes,' depending on the contribution of each person."[17] All relationships that matter (including this one) require attention. When we neglect them, they eventually dry up and wither. A garden left unattended will be overtaken by weeds. While this does not happen immediately, we make a huge mistake if we treat our relationships—with God or others—as static, as something merely given, the health of which can be taken for granted.

The contribution we make, what we put into the relationship, is a function of its authentic place in our minds and hearts. One does not become the bishop overnight. But it is the destiny, in one form or another, of all those who neglect the health of their relationship with God. Prayer, in the words of St. Teresa of Avila, is a "close sharing between friends," a matter of taking time to be with our Beloved (cited in *CCC* 2709). It is so important to "waste" time with those we love. This "wasting of time" together both reveals and grows our love.

If we don't tend to our relationship with God, we may find ourselves, like the bishop, in a situation quite far from where we began—and we might not even understand how we got there. The journey of faith is an ongoing pilgrimage. But patterns of neglect add up over time. As with any relationship, consistency in the little things makes all the difference, especially in prayer.

Prayer roots us more firmly in Christ and the truth of the faith so that "we may no longer be . . . tossed back and forth . . . with every wind of doctrine" (Eph 4:14). It is essential for growing in both dimensions of faith—helping us to make the abstract truths of the faith living realities with which we come into daily contact, and enabling us to courageously take the risk of faith by entrusting our lives to God in a profound and life-altering manner every single day.

THREE

The Relentless Grip of One's Ego

One of the first characters we encounter in *The Great Divorce* is the "Big Ghost" (or Big Man). He is met by Len from the mountain country, who worked under him earlier in life.[1] The Big Ghost is floored to see Len, because it turns out that Len had *murdered* another acquaintance of theirs named Jack. Len tries to explain that everything has now been set right.

The Big Ghost laments, "Aren't you ashamed of yourself?"

"No. Not as you mean," says Len. "*I do not look at myself. I have given up myself.* I had to, you know, after the murder. That was what it did for me. And that was how everything began."[2]

"My Rights"

Len's forgetting of himself is exactly what the Big Ghost needs to do, but it is something that proves very difficult. The Big Ghost insists that he has only ever asked for what he deserved, what was his by right, claiming he always did his best. Len encourages the Big Ghost not to go on about rights, but the Big Ghost won't let up, continuing to express his dismay at the fact that Len made it into the mountain country.[3]

As the Big Ghost carries on, Len makes it clear—this is not about rights: "Oh no. It's not so bad as that. I haven't got my rights, or I should not be here. You will not get yours either. You'll get something far better. Never fear."[4]

The Truth

The Big Ghost needs to let go of his "rights" talk and realize that he has deceived himself at various points along the way. Len explains, "You can never do it like that. . . . Your feet will never grow hard enough to walk on our grass that way. You'd be tired out before we got to the mountains. *And it isn't exactly true, you know.*"[5]

The Big Ghost retorts, "What isn't true?"

"You weren't a decent man, and you didn't do your best. We none of us were and none of us did."[6]

The Big Ghost is enraged at Len's words. But Len goes on to explain why he was the one sent to meet the Big Ghost. Len, like all those who worked under the Big Ghost, "murdered" their boss daily in their heart: "That is why I have been sent to you now; to ask your forgiveness and to be your servant as long as you need one. . . . But all the men who worked under you felt the same. You made it hard for us, you know. And you made it hard for your wife too and for your children." This, of course, infuriates the Big Ghost even more, as he tells Len to stay out of his "private affairs." But from heaven's standpoint, "There are no private affairs."[7]

Len promises the Big Ghost the joy of transformation if he continues into the mountain country. It will be painful and plenty of work, but there will be great joy once he becomes acclimated to the richness of the heavenly country. Len assures the Big Ghost of his support and service along the way. Yet the Big Ghost cannot surrender his pride; he will not take responsibility for his part in what he did wrong: "Tell them I'm not coming, see? I'd rather be damned than go along with you. I came here to get my *rights*, see?"[8]

We leave off with the Big Ghost saying that he is going "home," back to the grey town, as he whimpers at the pain of walking on the blades of grass. The grass is painful to those who are not *of* the mountain country, to those who have not been transformed by its radiance. The only way he can become like the mountain country is to let go of himself, surrender his pride, and continue the journey.

Pride

The theme of pride runs throughout several stories in *The Great Divorce*; it is known as the supreme deadly sin for a reason. Pride in this sense is certainly not the way we feel after working hard, as in "taking pride in one's work." Rather, pride is a stubborn clinging to our own will. It is what keeps us, for example, from apologizing at all costs. Pride keeps us from ever admitting fault, taking responsibility, and seeking forgiveness—from God and others.

In the story here, Len commits the more egregious crime externally. Yet, mysteriously, committing this act brought him face-to-face with himself, eventually bringing him to realize the wrongfulness not only of the murder but also of the seething anger that he had nurtured for years against the Big Ghost. But it is the Big Ghost—who committed no obvious and heinous external crime—who finds himself in the grey town. The Big Ghost seems to have been selfish and self-centered, insisting upon his own way, and apparently a difficult person to get along with, even for his own family.[9]

The stubborn willfulness to refuse wrongdoing, the refusal to repent and take responsibility, makes all the difference in this story. The Big Ghost is unwilling to see things from another point of view besides his own. This stubbornness keeps him from the glory of the mountain country—something not imposed from the outside, but coming from within.

It is hard and exacting work to own up to one's weaknesses and faults, the ways in which our words, actions, or inactions have brought pain into our relationships. It takes significant spiritual and moral effort to get past the myopic viewpoint of our own egos. But it makes all the difference in our relationships. We have likely known people who have done this successfully in our interactions with them, as well as those who have not. Herein lies the deciding factor of whether the Big

Ghost continues the journey into the mountain country; tragically, he chooses himself and his own pride over repentance and transformation.

Forgiveness

Jesus is deadly serious about forgiveness, even indicating that our being forgiven is contingent upon our forgiving others: "If you forgive others their transgressions, your heavenly Father will forgive you. But if you do not forgive others, neither will your Father forgive your transgressions" (Mt 6:14–15). Very often, our letting go of pent-up bitterness and resentment is the precursor to God's deeper healing within us. Our lack of forgiveness—and our lack of seeking forgiveness for what we have done—can become a spiritual block, preventing the Lord from working more deeply within our hearts. We know it is important, but entering into this work of forgiveness can be daunting, even seemingly impossible at times.

Robert Enright, a psychologist well known for his work on forgiveness, offers poignant observations from his clinical practice. For example, he describes how in his experience seething anger tends to stem from a consistent pattern of *minor* offenses, which accumulate over time: "Although a single painful event can lead to intense resentment, most smoldering resentments are caused by a series of small offenses."[10]

Over time, we develop a narrative in our minds, particularly about the other person's motives and why they seem to disregard our well-being. We say the other person is angering us for this or that reason. But in truth, it is not just the events that trigger us. It is the combination of the various events *and the story we generate in our own minds* about why they behave as they do that stirs such deep emotion within us (e.g., "they do this because they don't respect me" or "they don't care about my well-being").[11]

Our interpretive stories likely capture something of the truth—they generally don't come from nowhere. But it is also possible that our story is coloring the reality more than we realize, disposing us to interpret things in a more negative light. By engaging our feelings and even questioning our stories, we bring the depth of what is at play to light. According to the authors of the widely acclaimed *Crucial Conversations*, "We [should] challenge the comfortable conclusion that our story is right and true. We [should] willingly question whether our emotions (very real) and the story behind them (only one of many possible explanations) are accurate."[12] Maybe, just maybe, there's more to it; maybe the reality looks somewhat different—and even accurately so—from another person's point of view. Perhaps our narratives only capture *part* of the story. This internal process is a crucial step toward sincere forgiveness and opening up the possibility of reconciliation (or at least greater mutual understanding).

It takes an emotionally mature person to ask themselves sincerely if there is evidence that runs contrary to their own story, whether there are signs of goodwill that run against the narrative they have built up in their mind over the years. It takes tremendous strength to try to see things as best we can from another person's point of view, interpreting them in the most charitable light possible. Enright counsels:

> A good rule to follow is that if you feel terribly guilty, you probably were at fault, *and if you feel completely innocent and absolutely justified in your anger, there is a good possibility that you may not be.* At some point in the forgiveness process, you may want to seek forgiveness for the wrongs you have done, even if your wrongs are 1% of the problem and the other person's wrongs are 99% of the problem.[13]

The Big Ghost is pent-up with anger, bitterness, and a deep sense that his rights have been violated. He is out to defend himself and his ego at all costs, as if he were the quintessential victim. Sometimes, feeling like we are the victim subconsciously justifies in our minds and hearts our own aggressive tactics (perhaps in a passive-aggressive way, or by ignoring the other person as a way of punishing them with our silence). Claiming to be the victim (even if just internally) can be a way of concealing, at least to ourselves, the fact that we are partially to blame.

Len, a far more dramatic, public sinner than the Big Ghost, has let go of himself, his rights, and what he deserves. And paradoxically, the Big Ghost's unwillingness to open himself up and see things from someone else's point of view is precisely what closes him off from God's mercy and grace. This posture made the Big Ghost an emotional "cancer" of sorts, the opposite of an instrument of healing for those around him.

Jesus is the Divine Physician. He seeks to make us whole. So often, holiness is about reintegrating the fragmented and wounded pieces within us that are longing to be seen, known, and loved. These fragmented parts of ourselves lead to countless ways of coping, which are sometimes destructive to relational dynamics. As the saying goes, "Hurt people hurt people."

May we come to Jesus as we are, in all our weakness and bitterness. In the depths of prayer, may he reveal himself and his love to us; and may he reveal to us the truth about ourselves and our relationships—even the truths we find difficult and painful to accept (e.g., the subtle ways we have brought pain to relationships, even if we were first wronged). May Jesus reveal these truths to us before it is too late, while we have time to turn to him and mend our relationships with those closest to us.

While these relationships should be the most intimate, they can also become the most painful when they get off kilter. Sometimes we may even feel like they have become a lost cause because of so much painful history. Trust in Jesus. Healing, forgiveness, mutual understanding, and even reconciliation are always possible with his grace. But we must first let go of ourselves—and our stories—and let Jesus illumine the whole truth about our lives and our relationships.

FOUR

Humility and Ambition—What's a Christian to Do?

We all have gifts and talents, and we're all here for a reason; each of us has a unique part to play in the time given us. The requisite balance is to recognize, on the one hand, the paramount importance of each one of us and, on the other hand, to avoid taking our own sense of self-importance too seriously. When we take ourselves too seriously, our own aggrandizement becomes the chief goal, instead of the particular task appointed to us by divine providence. And if we fail to realize our dignity in God's eyes, we neglect our absolute unrepeatability—that we are truly willed by God "for a time such as this" (Est 4:14).

Lewis describes a famous artist from the grey town who engages with a particular "Spirit" in the afterlife (who also was an artist).[1] The artist is moved by the landscape of the mountain country and is eager to paint it. But the Spirit insists, "Looking comes first." Yet the artist is insistent and impatient, leading the Spirit to explain:

> When you painted on earth—at least in your earlier days—it was because you caught glimpses of Heaven in the earthly landscape. The success of your painting was that it enabled others to see the glimpses too. But here you are having the thing itself. It is from here that the messages came. There is no good *telling* us about this country, for we see it already. In fact we see it better than you do.[2]

The Spirit continues, "At present your business is to see. Come and see. He is endless. Come and feed. . . . If you are interested in the country only for the sake of painting it, you'll never learn to see the country."[3]

The artist has forgotten what drew him to his art in the first place. Over time, he came to seek art for its own sake, whereas initially his art was a means of unveiling the transcendent to others, to share with others the contemplative glimpse he had of the beautiful, of reality. The trajectory of the artist went from sharing his glimpse of the true and beautiful with others to art for its own sake, and thence to art for the sake of enhancing his own reputation and personal gravitas.

This attachment to his own self-importance and vanity is what the artist needs to overcome, an attachment that threatens to keep him from progressing toward the mountain country. Like the Big Ghost in the previous chapter, the artist must let go of himself—and trust that in this surrender, he won't lose himself but will find the fullness of himself in God.

The Spirit points to a fountain up in the mountain, reminiscent of the "living water" of the Gospel (see John 7:37–39; Ezekiel 47:1–12): "When you have drunk of it you forget forever all proprietorship in your own works. You enjoy them just as if they were someone else's: without pride and without modesty."[4] The Spirit's words "without pride and without modesty" are reminiscent of Lewis's teaching on humility elsewhere. The goal is not to belittle our accomplishments but to embrace the whole truth, recognizing our gifts and talents and giving credit where credit is due (not solely to ourselves, but to God and the people who have helped us along the way). True humility acknowledges the quality of our accomplishments, without putting the accent mark on the vanity of our egos and our yearning for approval and validation from others. Humility turns us outward and makes us receptive to the other, to God and neighbor. This virtue orients us toward reality itself, the very opposite of immersing ourselves solely in our own ego. In this way, our base self-love dies, resulting in a deeper and more authentic self-love.[5]

The artist is dismayed to hear the Spirit say, "Everyone will be interesting" and that nobody will be "distinguished" or famous. "The Glory flows into everyone, and back from everyone. . . . They are all famous. They are all known, remembered, recognized by the only Mind that can give a perfect judgment." The Spirit then informs the artist that even though they were both once well known on earth, now they are "already completely forgotten."[6]

This statement throws the artist into a panic. He cannot accept being forgotten, and he doesn't grasp how fleeting his reputation truly is. He sets off to "write an article," to "start a periodical," to regain some "publicity." And then he is gone. In fact, he "*vanished*."[7]

Let's be honest: How many of us know the names of our great-great-grandparents? After three or four generations, we, too, will most likely be forgotten. We cling to various things (reputation, monuments, accomplishments, children, and so on) as an attempt to overcome our mortality, our finitude. But the reality is that even *our own family's* memory of us will fade with the passing of a few generations. Though sobering, this is a lesson in what really matters. What is of the utmost importance is having our eyes on eternity and being faithful to the present moment passing before us (especially our relationships). For "here, we have no lasting city" (Heb 13:14). Unfortunately, the artist did not learn this lesson in life, and now in death it seems to be too late.

Made for Reality

God is the fullness of reality. He is the ground of all existence. He alone exists of his own accord; everything else shares in the gift of existence—participates in his gift of existence. To use an illustration, the milk in one's fridge does not have its own coolness; rather, it *participates* in the coolness of the fridge. Or, a metal rod in a fire does not possess its own heat; rather, it participates in the heat of the fire—sharing in a reality that it does not have by nature.

So, too, we (and all created things, including the highest of the angels) are not the source of our own existence. We participate in the "to be" of God. This is why St. Thomas Aquinas deemed the divine name (YHWH) revealed to Moses at the burning bush to be such a fitting and perfect name for God (see Exodus 3:14–15).[8] The root of this divine name is *hayah*, the Hebrew verb "to be." This is where we get the translations "I AM" or "I am who am." The Septuagint, the Greek Old Testament, translates this section of the Hebrew of Exodus as "I am he who is" (LXX, Ex 3:14, *ego eimi ho on*). This is why Jesus's "I am" statements are so alarming to his Jewish audience (see John 8:58), because he is taking the divine name of the God of Israel upon himself—he is claiming to be YHWH in the flesh.

We are made to encounter the real, made to encounter God, the source of all reality. *Truth* is simply reality apprehended by the intellect. *Goodness* is reality under the aspect of what is desirable and apprehended by the will. *Beauty*—the most mysterious of the transcendentals—can be seen as a combination of the true and the good together.[9] Reality, in other words, is what our human powers (especially intellect and will) are made to feast on. This thirst for the real is an inchoate thirst for God.[10]

All this postures us outward, with open hands, to receive the gift of reality—the reality of the world around us and especially the people around us. But the inward turn, the collapse of ourselves upon our egos, is the inverse of that for which we are made. To be absorbed by our own egos is to collapse into a *nothingness*. This is what Lewis is hinting at by saying that the artist "vanished" at his sudden realization of the fleetingness of his own reputation—that he had already been forgotten back on earth. When we worship ourselves, we collapse into an apparent nothingness. We are made for reality: to behold and enter into the creaturely participations of the true, good, and beautiful, and to unite ourselves to the Uncreated Good—God himself, who alone can satisfy the human heart and overcome the fleetingness of our existence.

St. Augustine: God or Nothing

In his *Confessions*, St. Augustine (354–430) recounts his own story in a similar way. He opens in prayer, recognizing that we are made for God: "You have made us and drawn us to yourself, and our heart is unquiet until it rests in you." He explains that his turn away from God and embrace of sin was a *turn away from reality*, leading to the loss of himself and a collapse into a sort of nothingness. "I will try now to give a coherent account of my *disintegrated* self, for when I turned away from you, the one God, and pursued a multitude of things, *I went to pieces*."[11] This is the nothingness of self-absorption.[12]

Our choice, in the end, is God or self. The choice of self—as with the artist above—makes us wither away. Indeed, what Lewis is driving at with the vanishing of the artist is that the choice before us is God or *nothing*. The latter is the choice of true nihilism, the self-centered absorption of our egos. This is what happens when we opt for that which is fleeting over the real—ultimately choosing sadness over joy.

FIVE

Well-Intended Dysfunction

As happens so often in Lewis's writings, the little things make all the difference, as they reveal and test one's character. In one example, Lewis introduces us to a female Ghost, who had been married to a man named Robert. The female Ghost is met by a Spirit from the mountain country named Hilda, who knew the couple earlier in life (and seems to have some relation to Robert).[1]

The female Ghost and Robert's marriage had been strained, and she is not eager to see him. In fact, she expresses surprise and dismay that Robert is already in the mountain country. She feels as though she was wronged in life and that she is the one who helped Robert become something. She is insistent, and part of the conversation consists of her interrupting and cutting off the bright spirit: "You haven't the faintest conception of what I went through with your dear Robert. The ingratitude! It was I who made a man of him! Sacrificed my whole life to him!'"[2]

The female Ghost goes on to lament Robert's laziness and how she had to coax him to take on extra work. One gets the sense that she suffocated Robert in a rather controlling manner:

> I used to spend hours arranging flowers to make that poky little house nice, and instead of thanking me, what do you think he said? He said he wished I wouldn't fill up the writing desk with them when he wanted to use it: and there was a perfectly frightful fuss one evening because I'd spilled one of the vases over some papers of his. It was all nonsense really, because they weren't anything to do with his work. He had some silly idea of writing a book in those days . . . *as if he could. I cured him of that in the end.*[3]

Robert's wife also sought to influence his social circle. She wanted him to have "useful" friends who could enhance his social status. "No more of his sort of friends, thank you. I was doing it all for his sake. Every useful friend he ever made was due to me."[4] Robert had a nervous breakdown toward the end of his life, seemingly a result of the disharmony within their home.

While the female Ghost initially did not want to meet her husband, she eventually warms up to the idea—but only if it means that she can continue "fixing" him. "I will *not* meet him, if it means just meeting him and no more. But if I'm given a free hand, I'll take charge of him again. I will take up my burden once more. . . . With all the time one would have here, I believe I could still make something of him." She continues, interrupting Hilda: "Please, please! I'm so miserable. I must have someone to—to do things to. It's simply frightful down there [in the grey town]. No one minds about me at all. I can't alter them."[5] Like the artist in the previous chapter, the female Ghost here shrivels up, seemingly into nothingness.

Virtue, Habit, and Reality

The beauty and power of the virtue tradition is that it captures how we are constantly in a state of becoming who we are, a process that becomes more fixed over time as our habits become ever more deeply ingrained, a "second nature," as it were. Virtues are like skills, the skills needed to live life with excellence. They function like skills in other areas, such as those of a craftsman, an athlete, or a musician. In each of these areas, it is not the doing of an isolated action that makes the person skilled. Rather, it is through the repetition of such acts over time that one becomes the kind of person who can perform such actions with excellence on a consistent basis. We possess a given virtue when we can perform it *consistently*, *promptly*, and *with joy*. Practice makes—if not perfect—more and more permanent, as the particular skill or virtue becomes an ingrained aspect of our character.[6]

This deep sense of becoming is so profound that *who we are* changes in the process of acquiring virtue. Over time, we alter our very selves. In the words of St. Gregory of Nyssa:

> Human life is always subject to change; it needs to be born ever anew . . . but here birth does not come about by a foreign intervention, as is the case with bodily beings. . . . It is the result of free choice. Thus *we are* in a certain way our own parents, creating ourselves as we will, by our decisions.[7]

We become our habits, as our most deeply ingrained character. This goes for both virtue and vice. The more we feed habits, the stronger they get. When vice, for example, becomes an ingrained habit, it takes over our lives, and we lose our freedom to love. The reverse is true for virtue, as this habit gives us a greater and more effortless freedom to love (and to love consistently and with greater joy). Over time, acting in a manner contrary to the way we have habituated ourselves feels unnatural. The more we become accustomed to a certain pattern of life, the stronger its gravitational pull—and the pace of our acceleration toward virtue or vice picks up steam as we go along.

Habituation to virtue makes us *expansive*, disposing us to enter more fully into reality (especially union with God and neighbor). As with the artist in the previous chapter and Robert's wife here, habituation to vice collapses us further and further into ourselves, toward nothingness and despair. It's as if vice has so overtaken these characters that *there is nothing else left*. Here, we get a glimpse of the *nothingness* of hell, when the soul is overcome by self-centeredness and self-absorption. Lewis writes:

> The whole difficulty of understanding Hell is that the thing to be understood is so nearly Nothing. But you'll have had experiences . . . it begins with a grumbling mood, and yourself still distinct from it: perhaps criticizing it. And yourself,

> in a dark hour, may will that mood, embrace it. You can repent and come out of it again. But there may come a day when you can do that no longer. Then there will be no *you* left to criticize the mood, nor even to enjoy it, but just the grumble itself going on forever like a machine.[8]

When we become ensnared by our own egos, we turn inward. The more entrenched the habit, the stronger this inward pull becomes. This is the opposite of becoming expansive, as we can no longer take in and receive reality—we are no longer poised outward to enter into loving union with God and neighbor. In the context of our relationships, as with the Big Ghost earlier, we are no longer able to see things from another's point of view, no longer able to get beyond ourselves and truly enter the world of another.

If love fully actualizes the person—fully brings about our enhancement through virtue—then our failure to love results in a lesser version of ourselves. We collapse into the black hole of our own ego. As love withers, *we wither*. This is the fate of the artist and of Robert's wife. No longer able to get beyond the vanity of their own ego (i.e., the artist) or the myopic vantage point of their own concerns and interests (i.e., Robert's wife), their self-centered gravitational pull has diminished them—to the point of their vanishing into the nothingness of hell.

We are made to get outside ourselves—made for the real. We are made for love.

In the next two chapters, we will explore the nature of authentic love more fully and the challenge Christian charity entails.

SIX

The Death and Resurrection of Love

Lewis introduces us to a mother Ghost named Pam, who is met by a bright spirit named Reginald (who is Pam's brother). Pam had lost her son, Michael, at a young age and remains heartbroken over her loss.[1] Pam is annoyed to be met by Reginald and asks why she is not greeted by her son. Reginald explains to Pam that Michael cannot see her yet—she will be invisible to him until she is built up (by progressing into the mountain country).

Disgruntled, Pam responds, "I should have thought if *you* can see me, my own son could!" Though a very difficult truth to hear, Pam is told that her love for her son had become distorted. Reginald explains, "You will become solid enough for Michael to perceive you when you learn to want Someone Else besides Michael."[2]

Pam responds indignantly, "You wouldn't talk like that if you were a mother."[3]

Reginald replies, "You mean if I were *only* a mother,"[4] since one is first a creature of God, even prior to being a mother.

Pam is understandably angry at God for taking Michael away. Indeed, we should be honest with the Lord when we are angry with him—and eventually we must seek to "forgive" him for what he allowed us to go through. While God has not actually wronged us (since he is all-good), it may feel very much like he has. For this reason, it is healthy (and holy) to work through our reconciliation with God and our acceptance of the suffering he has allowed for us. These are deep spiritual waters, which require serious prayer and often the help of counseling and spiritual direction (along with the support of family and friends). We must be honest with our anger toward God and our circumstances in our efforts to accept and embrace the fact that a loving mystery lies behind whatever divine providence has allowed us to undergo, trusting that his ways are not our own and that he has a plan far greater than we can see.[5] Yet, even accepting this truth by faith does not make it easy. This genuine "wrestling" with God is crucial to our healing and growth (see Genesis 32:22–30).

We get a glimpse of this mystery with Pam, when Reginald says, "But He had to take Michael away. Partly for Michael's sake. . . . And, secondly, for your sake. He wanted your merely instinctual love for your child . . . to turn into something better."[6]

At this point, we get a small window into how Pam's disordered love for her son impacted the rest of the family:

> The instinct was uncontrolled and fierce and monomaniac. (Ask your daughter, or your husband. Ask our own mother. You haven't once thought of *her*.) . . . No man ever felt his son's death more than Dick [Pam's husband]. Not many girls loved their brothers better than Muriel [Michael's sister]. It wasn't against Michael they revolted: it was against you—against having their whole life dominated by the tyranny of the past: and not really even Michael's past, but your past.[7]

Pam insists that she would be perfectly happy in the grey town (in hell) if she had Michael with her. She would rather have Michael with her even at the price of his misery. In response, Reginald poignantly states, "You cannot love a fellow-creature fully *till you love God*."[8]

This is a hard pill for those without faith to swallow. Is it right to put God ahead of family? Is it not the case that even many otherwise serious Catholics almost subconsciously invert this order—putting family above God (even if they *say* otherwise)? Putting God first, in both word and deed, is a more challenging task than we often realize.

The Secret to Holy Families

Let's try to understand what Lewis is getting at. To love someone is to will their good; this means that we will the other's happiness. But the nature of this love is more or less specific depending upon our clarity as to what the ultimate good is—our sense of what true happiness consists in. Is our conception of happiness merely relativistic ("whatever makes you happy"), or is it tied firmly to God and virtue?

In the words of the future pope St. John Paul II, to really love someone means we want the good "without limits" for them. Only people of deep faith realize that this means we want God for them. To truly love the other, then, is to will their union with God and to foster that union above everything else.[9] However, when we do not consciously make the connection between God and true happiness, willing the other's happiness easily takes on a relativistic flavor. We can develop a "love" for the other that is sympathetic to self-destructive behavior (e.g., alcohol, drugs, promiscuity), because we are willing to accept "whatever makes them happy," however they wish to define it.

Further, when our loves are not placed in God—in the overarching context of our journey back to God—we often seek our definitive happiness in and through creatures. Gradually, we begin to care less about the objective good of the other and more about our *experience* with the other. That is, even though we do not realize it, our love takes on a selfish tinge. This happens, for example, when parents elevate "being together" over what is objectively best for the child—an easy trap to fall into, as we miss the days when all the kids were young and under our roof. Sometimes—and this is perhaps *the* great cross of parenting adult children—we must love them enough to let them go. This is often the last great sacrifice we make for our adult children—placing their good and what God has called them to above whatever we may desire, even above our desire to be with them.

Indeed, the key to holy families is that the family is not an end in itself. Rather, the family's union is constituted fundamentally by their journeying together toward the final goal, heaven. Heaven becomes the ultimate end, not the family itself—not simply being together. This allows the family members to adjust their actions—even when painful—to stay in accord with their true end and that of each member. This is to place the family's love *in* God, in our journey back to him, which is exactly what Pam is finding it so difficult to do.

Even St. Monica, mother of the wayward Augustine, fell into this. St. Augustine recounts the time when he snuck off to Rome from Carthage, taking a ship by night, unbeknownst to his poor mother. Augustine recalls how God "took no heed" of what Monica was praying for at that moment—namely, that he would remain close to her and not depart. And yet in doing so, Augustine sees that God was actually answering her deepest prayer—that he would return to the Catholic faith, for it was through his journey to Rome and then Milan that he would encounter the great Bishop Ambrose and eventually make his way back to the faith of his youth:

> And what was she begging of you, my God, with such abundant tears? Surely, that you would not allow me to sail away. But in your deep wisdom you acted in her truest interests: you listened to the real nub of her longing and took no heed of what she was asking at this particular moment, for you meant to make me into what she was asking for all the time. . . . You took no heed, for you were snatching me away, using my lusts to put an end to them and chastising her too-carnal desire with the scourge of sorrow. *Like all mothers, though far more than most, she loved to have me with her*, and she did not know how much joy you were to create for her through my absence.[10]

When Pam insists that "mother-love" is "the highest and holiest feeling in human nature," Reginald responds, "Pam,

Pam—no natural feelings are high or low, holy or unholy, in themselves. They are all holy when God's hand is on the rein. They all go bad when they set up on their own and make themselves into false gods."[11] Every natural inclination or feeling must be purified to enter the mountain country. Every natural love must "die" to be born anew.

Another Natural Desire

The point that Lewis develops throughout this chapter is that no natural appetite or feeling can go to the mountain country as it currently is, no matter how noble; but every natural appetite or feeling—if it first submits to death—will be raised and transfigured anew in the glory of God's kingdom.

The more exalted in the natural order, the more easily the appetite or feeling can be mistaken for the real thing—and therefore, the more deceptive it can be. Indeed, the more exalted in the natural order, the more relentlessly the natural feeling or appetite tries to become its own end, subordinating everything else to its satisfaction.[12] This is why the good of family life—one of the most exalted of all natural goods—so easily becomes its own ultimate end. And this is what is happening with Pam's "mother-love," as she privileges her desire to be with Michael above all else.

Juxtaposed with the story of Pam and Michael in *The Great Divorce* is a story of a man with a lizard perched on his shoulder. The lizard stands for lust and the man hates it—yet he cannot get rid of it.

The man is approached by an angel from the mountain country who offers to kill the lizard. "'Would you like to make him quiet?' said the flaming Spirit."

"'Of course I would,' said the Ghost."

"'Then I will kill him,' said the Angel."

"'You're burning me. Keep away,' said the Ghost, retreating."[13]

The man vacillates back and forth, asking the angel for a more *gradual* process. But the angel insists, "There is no other day. All days are present now. . . . This moment contains all moments."[14]

"Get back! You're burning me," the man says.[15] The angel had promised that in killing the lizard, he would not kill the man—though he could not promise that the process would be without pain.

The angel cannot act against the man's will; the man must first consent. "I cannot kill it against your will. It is impossible. Have I your permission?"[16]

The lizard then begins speaking to the man, begging him to go against the angel's wishes: "I'll be so good. I admit I've sometimes gone too far in the past, but I promise I won't do it again. I'll give you nothing but really nice dreams—all sweet and fresh and almost innocent. You might say, quite innocent . . ."[17]

In the throes of his conversion, St. Augustine similarly describes his old vices speaking to him, beseeching him not to send them away, murmuring in his ear: "Do you mean to get rid of us? Shall we never be your companions again after that moment . . . never . . . never again? From that time onward so-and-so will be forbidden to you, all your life long."[18] Like Augustine, the man with the lizard eventually concedes to the mystery of grace and gives the angel permission, saying, "God help me. God help me."[19]

In St. Augustine's story, he hears another voice—Lady Continence (representative of Lady Wisdom and the Church)—beckoning him: "Cast yourself on him [God] and do not be afraid: he will not step back and let you fall." As Augustine places his trust in God, having recourse to St. Paul's letters (particularly Romans 13:13–14), he writes, "No sooner had I reached the end of the verse than the light of certainty flooded my heart and all dark shades of doubt fled away."[20]

In Lewis's *Chronicles of Narnia*, the character Eustace goes through a similarly dramatic transformation in *The Voyage of the Dawn Treader.* After having long been a snarky and disagreeable boy, through various twists and turns he gets himself turned into a dragon. But this process—this rock-bottom moment—initiates a renewal within him.[21] The climactic point of renewal comes about when Aslan (the Jesus figure in *Narnia*) *tears the dragon scales off Eustace*, bringing about a painful, yet liberating, transformation, analogous to the man with the lizard in *The Great Divorce.*[22]

What happens next in *The Great Divorce* is the most dramatic transformation of all: "Next moment the Ghost [the man with the lizard] gave a scream of agony such as I never heard on Earth. The Burning One [the angel] closed his crimson grip on the reptile: twisted it, while it bit and writhed, and then flung it, broken-backed, on the turf." Then the man undergoes a glorious metamorphosis:

> Then I saw, between me and the nearest bush, unmistakably solid but growing every moment solider, the upper arm and the shoulder of a man. Then, brighter still and stronger, the legs and hands. The neck and golden head materialized while I watched, and if my attention had not wavered I should have seen the actual completing of a man—an immense man, naked, not much smaller than the Angel.[23]

And then the lizard is simultaneously transformed as well:

> What distracted me was the fact that at the same moment, something seemed to be happening to the Lizard. At first I thought the operation had failed. So far from dying, the creature was still struggling and even growing bigger as it struggled. And as it grew it changed. Its hinder parts grew rounder. The tail, still flickering, became a tail of hair that flickered between huge and glossy buttocks. Suddenly I stared back, rubbing my eyes. *What stood before me was the*

> *greatest stallion I have ever seen, silvery white but with mane and tail of gold.*[24]

As the man is gloriously transformed and the petulant lizard becomes a magnificent stallion, the horse carries the man upward into the mountain country: "Then, still like a star, I saw them winding up, scaling what seemed impossible steeps, and quicker every moment, till near the dim brow of the landscape, so high that I must strain my neck to see them, they vanished, bright themselves, into the rose-brightness of that everlasting morning."[25]

The man and all his powers—including his sex appetite—have become like the mountain country. The entirety of his being is transformed, and he is now fit to enjoy the heavenly mountain country. He has become *like* the mountain country. He is now solid—full, as it were—and accustomed to his true homeland, but only after undergoing the "crucifixion" of his natural appetite. When nature cedes to the crucifixion of grace, our natural powers are not diminished but gloriously enhanced. This is the meaning of the venerated theological axiom *Grace presupposes, builds upon, heals, and perfects nature.*[26]

Our Capacity to Be Transfigured

There is a "potency" or capacity latent within human nature that yearns for the glorious transformation of grace. In divine providence, the natural order is not suppressed when taken up into the order of grace, but transfigured. In fact, this is the divine ordering of *reason to faith*, of the *Old Covenant to the New*, and of *nature to grace*. Each of the former possesses what the theological tradition calls an "obediential potency." This is an innate capacity within a thing to be elevated and fulfilled in a way beyond its natural powers, beyond anything accessible to it on its own terms. Obediential potency refers to the capacity of a thing to be elevated and transfigured by the power of God, all the while remaining the same in kind and not losing its natural integrity.

It remains what it is by nature, but now gloriously transformed and elevated by the power of divine grace, far beyond its own innate capacities.[27]

An analogy can be found in a stained-glass window: On its own, it possesses its own integral beauty and perfection. But now imagine the same stained-glass window *radiantly illumined by the sun*: With the sun's elevating rays, the stained-glass window exhibits a splendor and perfection beyond its own innate capacity (apart from the sun). And yet the sun's illumination of the stained-glass window does not take away from its own integral nature but transfigures it to new heights. This is analogous to God's elevation of our human nature by grace: We are elevated to heights unreachable on our own, and yet this elevated perfection is not foreign to our nature but actualizes its deepest capacity in the most sublime and transcendent way, only made possible by the power of God.[28]

In the italicized examples above (reason, Old Covenant, nature), we have a story in search of an ending. For example, human reason has discovered the immensity of the cosmos, even pointing to the need for a Transcendent Cause of the cosmos. But reason still trembles before unknown (and unknowable) mysteries, even in the natural order, especially regarding the inner life of this Transcendent Cause.[29] Only the mystery of faith reveals the inner triune life of God.

Similarly, already within the Old Covenant we have the expectation of a future "new covenant" (see Jeremiah 31:31–34). If the Old were meant to be permanent, why would it contain a prophecy of the *New* Covenant within its own texts?

And likewise, the order of nature (especially human nature) can teach us much about virtue. But it knows nothing of original sin and the prospects of overcoming the tyranny of death, nor can it know about the gift of the Spirit and the theological virtues of faith, hope, and charity. The order of nature knows nothing of the graced transformation and transfiguration of

Christ's humanity, manifest in the Transfiguration and the Resurrection. Here, we see the glorious transformation wrought by divine grace not only in our souls but in our bodies as well, as in Christ we overcome the "last enemy," death itself (1 Cor 15:26).

All of this shows God's plan to lead us from reason to faith, from the Old Covenant to the New, and from nature to grace. Yet, in all these examples, the lower is not abolished by the higher. Rather, the dignity of the lower remains and is elevated by the higher. Faith, for example, does not glory in the suppression of reason; instead, reason is purified and reaches new heights when informed by faith—beyond what it could have reached on its own terms. The New Covenant shows the even more exalted dignity of the Old by unveiling the inner typology at work, as the Old Covenant prepares for and prefigures the glory of the New. Our human nature—and the height of the virtue tradition—is not rejected by our life in Christ but is taken up into the deeper divine order of total self-giving love. Christ came "not to abolish, but to fulfill" (Mt 5:17). This is what we see in the man's transformation above, as his desire for the erotic is taken up into the *agape* of God; even the energies of his sexual appetite are not abolished but completely transfigured.

Reason ⟶ Faith

Old Covenant ⟶ New Covenant

Nature ⟶ Grace

Contrasting Pam and the Man with the Lizard

The man with the lizard happens to be the *only* character in *The Great Divorce* who explicitly continues the journey into the mountain country. All the others either turn back or stop where they are (or vanish). This raises the question of which attachments present the greatest obstacles to progressing into the mountain country—here, the contrast is between lust and disordered mother-love.

As mentioned earlier, nothing can go on to the mountain country without first submitting to death, without first undergoing purification and transformation. But no appetite will be left behind if it submits to death—that is, *everything* that submits to death will be raised anew.[30]

The juxtaposition of the man's lust and the mother's love for her son in this chapter certainly raises a hard question. Did Pam's mother-love really prove to be a greater spiritual obstacle to going to the mountain country than the man's lust? As the main character asks his teacher, "Am I to tell them at home that this man's sensuality proved less of an obstacle than that poor woman's love for her son? For that was, at any rate, an excess of *love*."[31]

George MacDonald, the main character's guide at this point in *The Great Divorce* (and a nineteenth-century writer who greatly influenced Lewis), responds firmly: "Ye'll tell them no such thing. . . . Excess of love, did ye say? There was no excess, there was defect. She loved her son too little, not too much. If she had loved him more there'd be no difficulty."[32]

As we have seen, Pam desires closeness with her son above all. This is not necessarily the same as desiring his good. In fact, she is willing to sacrifice his good as long as she can have him with her, even if it means taking him permanently to the grey town.[33] Though counterintuitive from her perspective, as MacDonald says above, she loves her son not too much, but too *little.*

MacDonald continues, "That kind is sometimes perfectly ready to plunge the soul they say they love in endless misery if only they can still in some fashion possess it."[34] The challenge of mother-love is different than lust. The man's lust was never going to fool him into thinking it was the real thing—lust is quite obviously a far cry from love. But Pam's mother-love—while objectively higher and more noble in the natural order than the sex appetite—is far easier to mistake for the real thing. It is much easier to mistake the closeness of affection for genuine love.

The lesson MacDonald (and Lewis) put forth, then, is this: If the lizard became such a grand stallion, what would be the *even more glorious transformation of mother-love*, if it were to turn itself to the glory of God and submit to its own sacrificial death?

God and Human Love

Lewis is arguing that we cannot fully love others unless we first love God and ultimately want the greatest good for our loved ones—God himself. All created goods (even the good of family life) are *participatory* goods: While truly good, they point beyond themselves to the Uncreated Good, to God himself. When finite goods become supreme in our lives, we choose the *gift* over the *Giver*, the creature over the Creator, which is the very essence of sin and idolatry, even if unbeknownst to us in the moment. Lewis writes: "There is but one good, that is, God. Everything else is good when it looks to Him and bad when it turns from Him. And the higher and mightier it is in the natural order, the more demoniac it will be if it rebels."[35]

Without God, our love exchanges the creature for the Creator, and we end up loving the creature *wrongly*—even in a way that's destructive for the creature in question. This is evident in Pam's love for Michael and her willingness to plunge him into hell so long as she can have him close. If we do not place our love for creatures *in* God, our love inevitably becomes disordered. As is the case with Pam, we then place our desired *experience* with the person above their objective good. This becomes a form of selfishness in disguise, as we are in effect loving ourselves through our experience with the other (even though this is usually quite far from our conscious awareness).

Encountering God in Others

Placing our love for creatures in God enables us to love them in a deeper and more unconditional way. This shows up in Karol Wojtyła's play, *The Jeweler's Shop*, particularly in act 2, "The Bridegroom," where we meet Anna and Stefan, a struggling couple. Their love has withered and grown cold and is on the verge of collapse. Stefan is unresponsive and emotionally distant, and Anna is preparing to run off with a stranger.[36] A mysterious character named Adam approaches and shows Anna a group of wise and foolish virgins, alluding to the parable in Matthew 25 (Adam seems to be symbolic of conscience or divine providence, though at points he is reminiscent of the role Wojtyła played in ministering to college students in Poland).

The foolish virgins are asleep. Here, sleep is a metaphor for spiritual and moral lethargy, something like the deadly sin of sloth. Adam has come to wake Anna, to draw her back to what life is all about: "To you it seems that they [the foolish virgins] are asleep . . . but in reality they too are walking down the street. They are walking in their sleep. They are walking in a lethargy—they have a dormant space in them. You now feel that space in you, because you too were falling asleep. I have come to wake you. I think I am in time."[37]

The Bridegroom (Jesus) is coming, and Adam tries to awaken Anna to get her ready to meet him. He explains that her yearning to be seen, known, and loved is at bottom a yearning for the love of the Bridegroom:

> You cannot live without love. I saw from a distance how you walked down this street and tried to rouse interest. I could almost hear your soul. You were calling with despair for a love you do not have. . . . Ah, Anna, how am I to prove to you that on the other side of all those loves which fill our lives—there is *Love!* The Bridegroom is coming down this street and walks every street! How am I to prove to you that you are the bride? . . . You would then hear him speak: beloved . . .

> how much you belong to my love and my suffering—*because to love means to give life through death.*

Anna reacts with horror when she finally encounters the Bridegroom. She shouts, "I have seen the face I hate."[38] For the Bridegroom has the face of her *husband*, Stefan.

We encounter the Bridegroom in and through the people closest to us, in and through the bonds of love interwoven in our path of life: "In the Bridegroom's face each finds a similarity to the faces of those *with whom love has entangled us on this side of life, of existence.* They are all *in him.*"[39]

Love of God and Love of Neighbor in Synthesis

To love creatures well, God must be central—in terms of our placing our loves *in* God and also, as here with Anna, by seeking to love God *in* those closest to us. Love of God and love of neighbor stand and fall together, mutually reinforcing each other. Only in this way do we find a true source of unconditional love—to love Jesus *in* our spouse and family.

This encounter with the Bridegroom breathes new life into Anna and provides a glimmer of hope for her marriage: "A new love could begin only through a meeting with the Bridegroom." Love is at the core of the meaning of life. But real love turns outward, never inward, as we've seen throughout *The Great Divorce.* It is about self-gift, never self-serving, and it draws its life from God. In turn, writes Wojtyła, authentic love offers the world a glimpse of the divine, because it "always reflects the absolute Existence and Love; it must always, *in some way*, reflect them. That, too, is the ultimate sense of your lives."[40]

Placing all our loves in God and encountering God in and through those closest to us is at the heart of Christian life. When God is removed, created goods are crushed under the weight of our longing. They can never fulfill us, even when we try to make them do so, as Pam attempts with her son. Loving creatures *in* God changes everything. Placing God at the center gives us the inspiration and the ability to love creatures better—to love Jesus *in* others, even when we find it difficult to do so. Only here do we have a true source of unconditional love, since the people we love the most will inevitably hurt us and let us down.

All of this is the lesson for both Pam and the man with the lizard (and for us). For Pam it is harder, because it might seem that mother-love is noble enough to run on its own, without any need for God. But such can never be the case. Mother-love is destined for glorious transformation, but only through its own "crucifixion." Otherwise, it, too, becomes a form of idolatry (even destruction and selfishness)—even if it *feels* like the real thing, as it surely did for Pam.

The man with the lizard also gives us hope. No part of us is beyond redemption, regardless of where we have been. God wants to forgive, heal, and transform us completely—not just our souls, but also our bodies. Christ enters the entirety of the human condition and makes us new. We need only say yes to his glorious work within us, and we, too, will become like the mountain country, our true home.

In the next chapter, we will continue our reflection on the nature of love by recourse to another set of characters in *The Great Divorce*.

SEVEN

Needy Love and Gift Love

So much of our discussion turns on the difference between loving another for how they make us *feel* versus loving them for *their own sake*, seeking above all what is objectively best for the other person.

In *The Great Divorce*, we read of a glorious procession, and the reader is thinking, "This must be the Blessed Mother!" But no, "Her name on earth was *Sarah Smith*."[1] The message is clear: In heaven, the glory of God redounds to everyone. None more so than the Blessed Mother, to be sure. And yet the most mundane person on earth will be gloriously radiant in heaven.

A dialogue takes place between Sarah Smith (sometimes called "the Lady") and "two phantoms," a "tall Ghost" (called the Tragedian) and a small Ghost (called the Dwarf), whom he seems to be leading.[2] But in fact, the little Ghost is leading the bigger one, at least initially. And it turns out that both ghosts are actually different aspects of *one* person named Frank.[3] The drama concerns which part of Frank will win out.

Frank and Sarah had been a couple earlier in life, and Sarah asks Frank for forgiveness. The Tragedian assents, assuming that Sarah must have been sad and heartbroken without him in the mountain country. Yet, sensing that Sarah has not missed him (at least not in the way Frank would like), he mournfully asks, "You mean—you did *not* love me truly in the old days?"[4]

Sarah responds in a manner that calls to mind the problems with Pam's love for her son in the previous chapter: "'Only in a poor sort of way,' she answered. 'I have asked you to forgive me. There was a little real love in it. But what we called love down there was mostly *the craving to be loved. In the main I loved you for my own sake because I needed you.*'"[5]

Frank is heartbroken over not being needed by Sarah. But as Sarah explains, now that she is full—completely filled with the love of God—she can love truly for the first time: "I am in Love Himself, not lonely. Strong, not weak. You shall be the same. Come and see. We shall have no *need* for one another now: we can begin to love truly."[6]

She pleads with Frank to let go of the chain, to send the Tragedian away: "It is *you* I want."[7] The Tragedian is now leading the charge in lamenting the fact that she no longer needs him and therefore does not love him.

The Lady appears to be getting the better of the exchange, reaching Frank's interior, as he seems to be "growing a little bigger," even "against his will." But the Tragedian eventually wins out, as the narrator tragically describes Frank's interior struggle. At this point, the Dwarf no longer speaks; only the Tragedian engages in dialogue with Sarah. She pleads: "'Don't, don't, Frank,' . . . 'Don't let it talk like that.' But the Dwarf was now so small that she had dropped on her knees to speak to it."[8]

Suddenly Sarah asks, "Where is Frank?" for the Tragedian has now fully taken over. At this point, the Tragedian is "very difficult to see."[9] Self-centered love has made him smaller, withering away. Then, like the artist and Robert's wife in previous chapters, the Tragedian *vanishes*, leaving Sarah alone in the mountain country.

The Nature of Love and Friendship

Although we use the word *love* in many ways, we mean very different things by it. For example: "I love ice cream." "I love my friends." "I love my family." "I love my country." "I love my God." Each of these uses indicates a somewhat different meaning of the word *love*.

Especially in the context of romantic love, Wojtyła distinguishes between "love as desire" and "love as goodwill" (or benevolence). As with Frank above, love as desire proceeds from a sense of *need*. It's a longing for the other *as a good for me*.[10] This is the nature of Frank's love for Sarah (and his desire for her to need him in the same way), as well as Pam's love for her son—her longing for her son to be near in some ways fulfills a need in her.

Love as goodwill or benevolence goes further by longing *for the other's good*.[11] This is a purer and more selfless form of love, and it's what Frank fails to understand and what Sarah tries to help him to see. It is also what Reginald sought to share with Pam.

For Wojtyła, love as desire and love as goodwill need not be at odds with each other, as they can be reconciled and integrated: "Let us say that [a man] wants [a woman] as a good for himself. In that case, however, he must want [her] to be good, since without this she cannot be a good for him."[12] In other words, if the other is going to be a real good for us (not merely an apparent good), they must become *good*—otherwise, they cannot be a true good for us. Therefore, in willing the good for another and helping to foster their true good, we actually help the other become a better good for us. In this way, Wojtyła sees the reconciliation of love as desire and love as goodwill.

Wojtyła distinguishes between true love and false love. The latter is detrimental to both parties, even though it may appear good or desirable, while "true love perfects the being of the person and develops his existence."[13] False love loves a true good but in the wrong way, in a way contrary to the other's true good. Pam turned to a true good (her son), but in a way that was opposed to his dignity as a child of God and his ultimate good. The same is true of Frank's love for Sarah. Sarah, in contrast, is now filled with the love of God in heaven and so is able to love Frank for the first time from a place of freedom—of gift—and not out of need.

Everything turns on what each person brings to the table. Do they bring gift love or needy (self-serving) love to the relationship? Do they seek the other merely to "fill them up," or are they zealously concerned for the objective good of the other?

In other words, what is the basis of their relationship? Is it merely the pleasure they enjoy by being together, "filling each other up" in that way? Is it merely that each person is advantageous or useful to the other? Or does their bond derive from their common pursuit of virtue? Our relationships are as deep as the good that binds us, as deep as the good we cherish and pursue together.[14] The nature of the reciprocal good upon which the relationship is based gives rise to the three traditional kinds of friendship: those based on *pleasure*, *utility*, and *virtue*.[15] The depth of the good upon which the relationship is based informs the stability and permanence of the bond. Friendships of pleasure or utility last only as long as each finds the other pleasurable or useful. When the pleasure or mutual advantage ceases, the bond loosens as well.

Virtuous friendship is "complete" friendship because it subsumes the other two. We should *enjoy* being around our virtuous friends, and they are *useful* in the most profound sense as partners in pursuit of the ultimate good. But virtuous friendship is *about something*, pursuing a transcendent goal together. It takes the bond deeper, building the relationship upon a more stable and enduring foundation. In a Christian context, this bond derives from a shared journey to heaven, union with Christ in this life and the next. Virtuous friends, then, sacrifice for each other to help each person reach their final end in Christ. Indeed, virtuous friends see the other's good as *their own*—the other's good becomes *our* good, as we become one mind and one heart.

The Anxiety of "Consumer" Love and the Security of "Gift" Love

Especially in a romantic setting, if each person brings only love as desire to the relationship, they bring a consumer mentality, with each person seeking what they can get out of the relationship. This makes the relationship only as secure as the emotional and physical satisfaction of each person, leading to distrust and anxiety. At best, this results in a harmonization of egoisms. But it cannot go further and is by nature unstable. It cannot rise to the level of genuine love. But, if each person brings love as goodwill to the relationship, they contribute something more. They aren't merely *taking*—they are *giving*, leading to a sense of mutual peace and trust. Life tests the integrity of every relationship; it tests the nature of the love that is "in" each person, and consequently what truly exists "between" them.[16]

In this sense, relationships are never static, as we pointed out earlier with regard to our relationship with God. Relationships are dynamic, and their growth (or regression) has everything to do with what each person brings to them, what kind of love they are contributing to the dynamism of the whole—a merely consumer love as desire, or true gift love oriented toward the good of the other. Wojtyła captures this well in a passage we mentioned earlier: "Love in a sense never 'is,' but only constantly 'becomes,' depending on the contribution of each person."[17]

As we said at the outset of this chapter, the great challenge of love is to move beyond loving the other for how they make us feel and come to love them for their own sake. Romantic love always begins with desire, but it cannot stop there. If we stop there, we are merely loving ourselves through our experience with the other—merely engaging in self-love in disguise. The danger, according to Wojtyła, is that the person becomes "less the object and more the *occasion*" for us to have a certain experience.[18] As we saw with Pam, the *experience* becomes primary (the experience of having her son close), not the other person and their true good. While this easily happens in a romantic setting, it can occur in other relationships as well, as we have seen with Monica and Augustine and Pam and Michael.

The heart of what Wojtyła calls "sinful love" is privileging our affective/emotional experience *above* the other person and their true good:

> Sin is then born from the fact that man does not want to subordinate affection to the person and love, but on the contrary, he subordinates the person and love to affection. "Sinful love" is often very affective; it is saturated with affection, which supplants everything else in that love. Of course, its sinfulness does not lie in the fact of being saturated with affection; it does not lie in affection itself, but in the fact that the will *places affection before the person*, and this cancels all objective laws and principles that must govern the union of persons, of a woman and a man.[19]

This is the challenge of love. True love comes by way of the Cross, sacrificing for the good of the other. Herein, needy love is transformed into gift love. As with the various natural appetites of the previous chapter, the purification and transformation of love as desire results in the elevated love of goodwill, true gift love. Sarah is prepared to love Frank in a way vastly superior to the love Frank claims to have for Sarah, because she is filled with the love of God and no longer turns to Frank out of need. Now she can become gift. Frank, on the contrary, starving for the love of God, turns to Sarah out of need, desiring her to "fill him up," so to speak, and is saddened that she no longer "needs" him in the same way.

So much of Lewis's and Wojtyła's writings aim to unpack this very tension. So many of our relationships turn on this issue. Will we allow Christ to purify our loves? Or will our appetite reign supreme, so that we end up using people for our own selfish ends—often under the guise of "love"?

Becoming *More*

Paradoxically, especially in the context of *The Great Divorce*, surrendering our appetitive desires—whether physical or emotional—to real love and the objective good of the other is the very means by which *we become more*. This crucifixion of sorts is how we become fit for the mountain country. Conversely, succumbing to our desires and allowing them to override the moral order and the objective good of the other is precisely how we become *less*, smaller on the inside, making us fit for the grey town and destined for misery. Gift, joy, and communion hang together—and their native habitat is the mountain country.

We turn next to consolidate all that we have gained from *The Great Divorce* to distill what Lewis is teaching about the nature of the afterlife and what heaven is really like.

EIGHT

What Is Heaven Like?

We have seen glimpses throughout this book of the vast difference between the grey town and the mountain country. When the people get off the bus, as we have noted, they are referred to as "ghosts" or "phantoms" because they are almost nothing in comparison to the mountain country and its inhabitants.

In the grey town, it is always "evening" and raining, while the mountain country is marked by the perpetual dawn of morning. The grey town is empty and isolated, with people moving apart just by *thinking* it. It is also without hope—the very opposite of the radiant communion and joy of the mountain country.[1]

As the people get off the bus, they notice that "the grass did not bend under their feet" because the new country is so much more substantial than they are, leading the main character to make this observation: "The men [getting off the bus] were as they had always been; as all the men I had known had been perhaps. It was the light, the grass, the trees that were different; made of some different substance, *so much solider than things in our country* that men were ghosts by comparison." Initially, the main character tries to pick up a daisy and "lost most of the skin" off his hands. As he tries to pick up a leaf, he states, "my heart almost cracked with the effort, and I believe I did just raise it. But I had to let it go at once; it was heavier than a sack of coal." Another oddity in this new world of the mountain country is that he can see the grass "not only between my feet but *through* them. I also was a phantom."[2]

Conversely, the "bright people," or the Spirits from the mountain country, are akin to the mountain country. They appear radiant and ageless. Not only can they walk effortlessly upon the terrain, but the earth rumbles under their feet:

> I saw people coming to meet us. Because they were bright I saw them while they were still very distant, and at first I did not know that they were people at all. Mile after mile they drew nearer. The earth shook under their tread as their strong feet sank into the wet turf. A tiny haze and a sweet smell went up where they had crushed the grass.[3]

At one point, a man is trying to bring apples from this new country back to the grey town. Because of their weight and grandeur, he gives up on the idea of taking several, thinking "two would have to do." Yet two are too heavy, so he decides to take just the largest one—a plan that he soon abandons, thinking he'll have to settle for the "smallest one." Eventually, a bright angel says to him, "Fool, put it down. You cannot take it back. *There is not room for it in Hell.* Stay here and learn to eat such apples. The very leaves and the blades of grass in the wood will delight to teach you."[4]

She Couldn't Fit

When the main character asks his teacher (George MacDonald) why the Lady (Sarah Smith) didn't go back to the bus with Frank—why she didn't journey all the way back to the grey town with him—his teacher points to a crack in the soil. He explains that their mysterious bus ride *was not a mere change of place.* Rather, the whole journey of the bus was a process of becoming like the mountain country—of dramatically changing in size and dimension. In fact, a mere crack in the soil is exactly what they came *through* to get where they are. The implication is that it would be impossible for Sarah Smith and the people of the mountain country to travel to the grey town:

> My Teacher gave a curious smile. "Look," he said, and . . . plucked a blade of grass. Using its thin end as a pointer, he made me see, after I had looked very closely, a crack in the soil so small that I could not have identified it without this aid. "I cannot be certain," he said, "that this *is* the crack ye

> came up through. But through a crack no bigger than that ye certainly came."

The main character is aghast, for he thought that he had traveled a great distance on the bus. "Aye. But the voyage was not mere locomotion," his teacher explains. "That bus, and all you inside it, were increasing *in size*."[5] The change was *qualitative*, not a matter of merely traveling from one "place" to another.

"Do you mean then that Hell—all that infinite empty town—is down in some little crack like this?" the main character asks.[6]

Yes, his teacher explains. Heaven is more *real* than hell—and far more real than anything on earth: "All Hell is smaller than one pebble of your earthly world: but it is smaller than one atom of *this* world, the Real World. Look at yon butterfly. If it swallowed all Hell, Hell would not be big enough to do it any harm or to have any taste." The man now sees the answer to his question plainly: "I see. . . . She [Sarah Smith] couldn't *fit* into Hell." His teacher continues:

> A damned soul is nearly nothing: it is shrunk, shut up in itself. Good beats upon the damned incessantly as sound waves beat on the ears of the deaf, but they cannot receive it. Their fists are clenched, their teeth are clenched, their eyes fast shut. First they will not, in the end they cannot, open their hands for gifts, or their mouth for food, or their eyes to see.[7]

How We Shut Ourselves Off from Joy

The Great Divorce shows a progression from the grey town to the mountain country. As we have noted, the grey town is hell for those who stay and purgatory for those who leave.[8] In this way, the grey town recalls the exile of God's people in the Old Testament. On the one hand, the exile is a covenant death of sorts, as the people are kicked off the Promised Land and removed from God's indwelling presence in the Temple (i.e., something like the eternal death of hell). On the other hand, the exile is also a matter of covenant discipline, calling the people back to repentance. In this way, the exile is a purifying and even atoning process that brings about spiritual renewal (i.e., something akin to purgatory).[9]

In *The Great Divorce*, several gradations emerge regarding the grey town and the mountain country:

- Deep Heaven (the inner heart of the mountain country)
- Valley of the Shadow of Life (for those journeying into the mountain country)
- Vallow of the Shadow of Death (for those getting off the bus and considering a journey into the mountain country)
- Hell (grey town)

In Lewis's work, the journey is retrospective. The people make their choice whether to continue into the mountain country in accordance with the dispositions and habits they have built up earlier in life. Hence, the process of journeying into the mountain country or imprisoning themselves in the grey town began long ago. What happens in the stories of *The Great Divorce* is simply a ratification of the way people have long positioned and habituated themselves. It is a ratification of what they have *become*. MacDonald explains:

> Ye can get some likeness of it if ye say that both good and evil, when they are full grown, become retrospective. Not only this valley but all their earthly past will have been Heaven to those who are saved. Not only the twilight in that town, but all their life on Earth too, will then be seen by the damned to have been Hell. . . . Both processes begin before death. . . . And that is why, at the end of all things, when the sun rises here and the twilight turns to blackness down there, the Blessed will say, "We have never lived anywhere

> except in Heaven," and the Lost, "We were always in Hell." And both will speak truly.[10]

"Hell," states MacDonald, "is a state of mind." As we have mentioned throughout, the people who turn back to the grey town turn inward upon themselves. They will not let go of their own egos—their stubborn attachments, their reputations, their desire to be loved and needed in the precise way they desire: "Every state of mind, left to itself, *every shutting up of the creature within the dungeon of its own mind*—is, in the end, Hell."[11]

Yet, heaven is no mere state of mind: "Heaven is reality itself. All that is fully real is Heavenly." And those that decline heaven's offer always have "something they insist on keeping even at the price of misery. *There is always something they prefer to joy*—that is, to reality."[12] The people who turn back to the grey town prefer themselves and their attachments to the joy of ever-expansive, self-giving love.

When all is said and done, there are two kinds of people, says Lewis: "Those who say to God, 'Thy will be done,' and those to whom God says, in the end, '*Thy* will be done.'"[13] It is the choice of self—or letting go of ourselves and our attachments. Surrendering the fallen part of ourselves is to choose joy, love, and ultimately God.[14]

The Beauty of Purgatory

Purgatory, for Catholics, is not a halfway house or a second chance after death. Purgatory is about God completing his work of healing and transformation in us, a work he begins on earth and will complete after our death if this healing and transforming work remains unfinished. This comes through beautifully in *The Great Divorce*, especially when the man with the lizard receives such a majestic transformation. Not only is the man forgiven upon his repentance, but he is thoroughly transformed. Even his sex appetite (formerly represented by the lizard) becomes a great stallion. Lewis is here signaling that every aspect of our lives will be transfigured by Christ. God's work does not end merely with our forgiveness. He seeks our complete healing and transformation—that's what the journey into the mountain country is all about. While initially painful, the journey is rehabilitative and transformative, as the people become *like* the mountain country.

"Nothing unclean shall enter [heaven]" (Rv 21:27). Any vestige of sin remaining within us will hinder our experience of joy and communion with God. Purgatory is all about the final burning away of our dross, enabling us to unite ever more closely with our all-holy God.

Importantly, purgatory is for the *redeemed*, for those who die in friendship with Christ, but are not yet fully purified and transformed: "All who die in God's grace and friendship, but still imperfectly purified, are indeed assured of their eternal salvation; but after death they undergo purification, *so as to achieve the holiness necessary to enter the joy of heaven*" (*CCC* 1030, emphasis added).

Purgatory makes us fit for heaven, so that we can enter thoroughly into the fullness of joy. It is the mudroom to heaven, as it were. It is the final workout—the final round of spring training—making us ready to enjoy *in the fullest way possible* the real season of our lives, our eternal life with God.

Even after our sins have been forgiven, the wounds of sin remain. Consider the image of a nail driven into a piece of wood. Let the removal of the nail signify forgiveness. Even after the removal of the nail, there is a hole in the wood. Catholics speak of the *eternal* and *temporal* consequences of sin. The former concerns forgiveness—am I repentant or not? This is what determines our fate—heaven or hell. Forgiveness is signified by the removal of the nail. The hole that remains signifies the *temporal* consequences of sin—the vestiges of sin that remain, even after we have been forgiven (see *CCC* 1472). The healing and transformation on display in *The Great Divorce* (especially with the man and the lizard) are what purgatory is all about.[15]

Those who reject purgatory fail to see the importance of the temporal consequences of sin and God's desire to completely transform us, to overcome any residue of sin remaining within us. Salvation is not merely a juridical decree; it is not merely forgiveness of sins, or a get-out-of-jail-free card. Salvation is about *divine sonship* in Christ, becoming a son or daughter in and through Christ and becoming totally conformed to him through the power of the Spirit (see Romans 8:29). The Christian life is a participation by grace in what the Son has by nature. While forgiveness is the necessary condition for our divine sonship, the gift of divine sonship vastly transcends the mere forgiveness of sins.

Purgatory is simply a matter of God completing the work he has begun in us in this life. Purgatory is all about the inherent dynamism of God's love, a love that loves us exactly as we are but too much to leave us that way—a love so powerful that it burns away our impurities and makes us radiant with divine glory and totally conformed to Christ.

Though not Catholic, Lewis conveys the truth of God's transformative love in *The Great Divorce*, capturing the essence of purgatory. He also hints at this in *The Screwtape Letters*. There, after the man in the story dies, he sees Christ, the angels, and even the demon who had been tempting him. And then Lewis offers this cryptic remark: "Pains he may still have to encounter, but they *embrace* those pains. They would not barter them for any earthly pleasure."[16] The "pains" that precede the man's eternal salvation seem to be an allusion to something like purgatory, something akin to the transformative pain of journeying into the mountain country.

The Great Divorce captures how we should think of these "pains," as it hurts the people to walk on the grass of the mountain country initially because they are not accustomed to the new terrain. The pain is not so much punitive as it is rehabilitative and transformative—much like the burn of a workout. Catholics sometimes focus too much on the punitive aspect (as well as on the "time" element) of purgatory.[17] There is tremendous *joy* in purgatory because everyone there is heaven bound. Purgatory is indeed the mudroom to heaven, the final preparation for the great banquet. As such, purgatory fits nicely into God's plan of salvation—to make us fallen sinners into glorious creations, radiant and infused with his very life. It is an expression of his plan to heal us and make us new. "Work out your own salvation with fear and trembling," says St. Paul, "*for God is at work in you*" (Phil 2:12–13, emphasis added).

"As fire transforms into itself everything it touches, so the Holy Spirit transforms into the divine life whatever is subjected to his power" (*CCC* 1127). Purgatory is the final burning away of any vestige of sin, any self-centered part of us that cannot remain if we are to enter into the fullness of this glorious communion, "*so as to achieve the holiness necessary to enter the joy of heaven*" (*CCC* 1030, emphasis added).

Longing for Heaven

Eternal rest means *no more restlessness*.[18] It does not mean "a really long time" or extended idleness. Eternal rest is the fullness of communion. We get a taste of this when we get lost in something we thoroughly enjoy; such a state is almost beyond time, and that's why we're surprised by how much time has gone by when we step away from some treasured activity.

Imagine being truly and authentically *seen*, *known*, and *loved*. Imagine no more misunderstandings or miscommunication, no more leftover baggage from years of small tensions and emotionally laden narratives built up in people's minds and hearts about us and our true intentions—all the things that break down honest dialogue and heart-to-heart communion. Imagine being fully understood, with all the masks removed, with no more defensive coping mechanisms preventing us from truly getting close to one another. This is the *intimacy* for which we long. This is the reality of heaven. This experience will be an "eternal *wow*," mesmerized by the beauty of the Father, Son, and Holy Spirit and the transfigured glory of his life pouring through each one of us, along with all the angels and saints.[19] This is the communion of saints, the intimacy for which our hearts long.

Everything we cherish the most in this life—those brief moments of joy and genuine communion—are but a foretaste of something greater to come. As the Old Testament prefigures the New (e.g., Eve and Mary, see *CCC* 128–129), so all that is true, good, and beautiful in this life prefigures something greater to come in heaven. To think that we will be bored in heaven is like a child thinking they'll be bored when they grow up—they just don't know any better. But if we think typologically—seeing the very best of this life as the appetizer to heaven—we can make better sense of our heart's infinite desire. The finite goods of this life, especially the ones we cherish the most, point beyond themselves to the next life. While we should enjoy them here, we must also learn to appreciate how they serve to whet our appetite for the life to come.

Life is a pilgrimage to the heart of the Father. As *The Great Divorce* displays so well, we are changed along the way—changed by the journey into his very likeness, so that we can enter into the fullness of his joy, without end. Let us close here by returning to Lewis's words from *Mere Christianity*, which capture this dynamic so well:

> If I find in myself a desire which no experience in this world can satisfy, the most probable explanation is that I was made for another world. If none of my earthly pleasures satisfy it, that does not prove that the universe is a fraud. Probably earthly pleasures were never meant to satisfy it, but only to arouse it, to suggest the real thing. If that is so, I must take

> care, on the one hand, never to despise, or be unthankful for, these earthly blessings, and on the other, never to mistake them for the something else of which they are only a kind of copy, or echo, or mirage. I must keep alive in myself the desire for my true country, which I shall not find till after death; I must never let it get snowed under or turned aside; I must make it the main object of life to press on to that other country and to help others to do the same.[20]

Everything in this life is a "sacrament," or sign of the life to come. While we cherish the earthly sign, we recognize that to which the sign points. As we do so, the beauty of this life becomes the great teacher of the life to come, beckoning us toward our final homeland.

In the next chapter, following Lewis's discussion in *The Great Divorce*, we reflect on the relationship between time and eternity, between God's eternal vantage point and our working through our own stories in real time and what this means for our life of faith.

NINE

Time and Eternity

George MacDonald introduces Christ's descent into hell toward the end of *The Great Divorce*. As the Lady (Sarah Smith) in the previous chapter couldn't fit in the "crack in the soil" to get back to the grey town, MacDonald explains, "Only the Greatest of all can make Himself small enough to enter Hell. For the higher a thing is, the lower it can descend—a man can sympathize with a horse but a horse cannot sympathize with a rat. Only One has descended into Hell."[1]

Like the Resurrection, Christ's descent into hell is a transcendent event, touching all times and all people: "All moments that have been or shall be were, or *are*, present in the moment of His descending. There is no spirit in prison to Whom He did not preach."[2] Here we have the intersection of time and eternity, of God's action in history in a manner that touches all history. The way in which the eternal God interacts with his finite and temporal creation is the greatest of mysteries.[3]

Drawing from Lewis and the Christian tradition, we turn now to discuss how our lives are eternally present before God even as we experience the drama of our lives unfolding in real time, and what this means for our spiritual journey.

The Eternal Now

To say God is "eternal" is not to say that he has been around for a very long time. The "e" in "eternal" is a negation—like when we say a particular plant reproduces *a*sexually. To be eternal is not to be timebound, that is, to be time*less*. In our experience, time is wrapped up with material things that change, giving us a clear sense of "before" and "after." That which is not material and not changeable, then, is not bound up in time. But notice, we are not saying anything positive. We are simply negating of God (*e*ternal, *un*changeable, *im*material) what can only be properly said of finite material creatures (that they are temporal, changeable, material).

This is why St. Thomas Aquinas says that all things—past, present, and future—exist in the "eternal now" of God.[4] Existing beyond and outside of time, God does not have tenses; he is everywhere present—not just in every space, but in every *time* as well.

But how can this be? And how can this be in such a way that does not take away our freedom? One of my favorite images for shedding light on this mystery is that of an author and a novel. For example, J. R. R. Tolkien is in a mysterious way present to the entirety of *The Lord of the Rings*. He is outside the story and is timelessly present to every moment of the story and every character within it. The characters within the story, of course, do not have this same experience. They are nervously working out Tolkien's plot in real time, as they struggle against their own weariness and the forces of evil around them. Surrounded by doubt, confusion, and strife, they struggle to maintain hope. But for Tolkien, their struggle makes them into who they are and who they are becoming, something that would never fully come about *without* their struggle. I like to envision Tolkien (and God) smiling at the perseverance and transformation of each character, as they embrace the reality of adventure, the drama unfolding before them—all fraught with a potentially perilous ending still unknown to them.[5] But in Tolkien's narrative (and in God's providence), there's a story—a plan—unfolding, even when it doesn't feel like it to the individual characters.

The world is like a book—God's book. We are characters in this great story, and we have a part to play. As we struggle through our own roles in the story, we have a deep sense of not knowing our fate—not knowing precisely how our stories will end. The full breadth of our lives does not appear within our horizon, even though it is entirely present to God. Our stories unfold in time. He sees from eternity, his eternal now.[6]

The amazing thing is that in Christianity, *God enters his own story*—as a character—in the Incarnation. Time and eternity intersect in God becoming man. The events of Christ's life—especially his death, descent into hell, Resurrection, and Ascension into glory—touch all times and all places. The life of Christ reveals *in time* what the life of the Eternal Son (and the entire Trinity) is like from all eternity. Our connection to Christ, then, bridges the gap between time and eternity, something we enter into most fully through the Sacred Liturgy, especially the Holy Eucharist, where the Paschal Mystery of Christ's death and Resurrection is made ever present.[7]

When God Feels Absent

Sometimes in our struggle, we can question despairingly, "Why would God allow me to go through this—and why does he seem absent?" We have all been there before. But if we consider the Tolkien analogy above, we see how God can be truly present to the story and yet feel absent to the individual characters. He sees at once the entire movement of our lives—our struggles, dips into discouragement, and (hopefully) our triumphant perseverance to the end. He is not absent, but present in so profound a way that we may be unaware he's there—just as the characters within a story are unaware of the constant and overarching presence of their author.

For me, to think of God as present to my whole story, all at once, gives me greater perspective. He sees a vision I cannot fully see, especially in my darkest moments. I only see one fragment at a time, one scene at a time, as is the case with the limited perspective of each of Tolkien's characters. At any given moment, they see only partial glimpses of the story. But we as readers—and even more with Tolkien as the author—stand outside the timeline of the story and see the whole all at once.

That is like the perspective of eternity; that's how God sees us. We know we cannot fully understand God's ways. But taking seriously the finitude of our perspective, bound as it is within time, can fuel our trust that there is more to the story than we experience from moment to moment. This awareness can galvanize us in the bleakest of times, especially when we feel like it's pointless to continue.

What Matters Most

What matters most is the gift of the present moment. It is only in the present moment that we experience the intersection of time and eternity. It is only in the present moment that we truly encounter God. In some ways, the past doesn't exist, save in one's memory.[8] Our past sins and accomplishments are not nearly as significant as the present moment. And the future is even more nebulous than the past—it is even more open-ended and indeterminate and therefore even less real. In *The Screwtape Letters* (through the voice of a fictional demon), Lewis explains that the demonic forces want us preoccupied with the future (or the past), and decidedly *not* with the present (or with eternity):

> Our business is to get them away from the eternal, and from the Present. With this in view, we sometimes tempt a human, say a widow or a scholar, to live in the Past. But this is of limited value, for they have some real knowledge of the past and it has a determinate nature and, to that extent, resembles eternity. It is far better to make them live in the Future. . . . It is unknown to them, so that in making them think about it we make them think of unrealities. In a word, the Future is, of all things, the thing *least like* eternity. It is the most completely temporal part of time—for the Past is frozen and no longer flows, and the Present is all lit up with eternal rays.[9]

The present is where our hearts are won or lost, where we are growing in our relationship with God and authentic love or collapsing in on ourselves. In the present, we can say yes to joy and communion—or we can turn inward upon ourselves.

When we recognize that all is gift—our time, our bodies, our very selves—we are more disposed to ask why the Author of all things has us where he does in this particular moment. We are more disposed to be attentive to the movements of the Spirit and entertain what mystery may be knocking at our door when people around us are in need or seem inconvenient to us, or when things seem not to be going our way.[10] When we see that all is gift, we are more inclined to make a gift of our lives and enter the stream of divine love in the present moment.

St. John Paul II captures this in a letter he wrote to one of the college students he ministered to in Communist Poland as she entered the next stage of her life, explaining what he saw as the divine logic of love: Those who need us the most bring out a greater love in us—and that's precisely why we need *them* as well:

> I am convinced that the (objective) starting point of love is the realization that I am needed by another. The person who *objectively* needs me most is also, for me, *objectively*, the person I most need. This is a fragment of life's deep logic, and also a fragment of trusting in the Creator and in Providence. . . . The great achievement is always to *see* values that others don't see and to *affirm* them. The even greater achievement is to *bring out* of people the values that would perish without us. In the same way, we bring out values in ourselves.[11]

Life is about love—communion through total self-gift. Through our experience of genuine finite love, we get a glimpse of the infinite love standing behind the universe, the love for which we are made. In Wojtyła's *The Jeweler's Shop*, as we saw earlier, Adam explains to Anna that behind all our efforts to grasp love in this life lies a thirst for something greater: "Ah, Anna, how am I to prove to you that on the other side of all those loves which fill our lives—there is *Love!*"[12] Earthly love is a sign of something more, pointing beyond itself to divine love.

And as cited earlier, Adam explains to Anna, "In the Bridegroom's face each of us finds a similarity to the faces of those *with whom love has entangled us on this side of life*, of existence. They are all in him."[13] We find Christ in the present moment. Our path back to God is through all those with "whom love has entangled us on this side of life." Real life is never *elsewhere*. It is ever before us—in the gift of the present moment, in the love to which Love beckons us.

May we prefer nothing whatever to joy, nothing whatever to Christ.[14] For therein, in the present moment, lies the dramatic battle of our lives. As the angel told the man with the lizard, "This moment contains *all* moments."[15]

And may we find Christ in loving the very people whom God has most directly put in our path, the very people whom we sometimes find it most difficult to love. This is the true meaning and legacy of our lives. In the end, nothing else matters. The only definitive tragedy is not to be a saint. Choosing against love is to choose against joy. Choosing against love is to choose ourselves and the nothingness such a choice brings. God or self—*God* or *nothing*—that is the choice of our lives.

We turn next to apply the lessons of *The Great Divorce* by considering two paths: the way of death and the way of life, outlined in Scripture and by our Lord himself (see Matthew 7:13–14). These two ways are manifested in the deadly sins and their opposing virtues, two diametrically opposed paths that draw out the choice Lewis puts before us in *The Great Divorce*: the self-centered turn inward, resulting in our collapse into an abyss of nothingness; or the outward turn toward reality and self-giving love. One brings death—the other, the fullness of life.

TEN

The Way of Death and the Way of Life

There is a deep biblical tradition of *two ways*, embodied in the two primordial trees of Eden, the tree of the knowledge of good and evil and the tree of life. Psalm 1 draws on this theme, contrasting the way of the righteous and the way of the wicked. The righteous are stable and flourish "like a tree planted by streams of water," with leaves that do not wither (Ps 1:3). The wicked are unstable "like chaff which the wind drives away" (Ps 1:4). The Lord *knows* (intimately) the way of the righteous, "but the way of the wicked will perish" (Ps 1:6).

This is also at the heart of Moses's final speech to the Israelites before they enter the Promised Land: "See, I have set before you this day *life* and *good*, *death* and *evil*. . . . Choose life that you and your descendants may live" (Dt 30:15, 19, emphasis added). And it is at the core of Jesus's teaching about eternal life and death: "Enter by the narrow gate; for the gate is wide and the way is easy, that leads to destruction, and those who enter by it are many. For the gate is narrow and the way is hard, that leads to life, and those who find it are few" (Mt 7:13–14).[1]

The deadly sins embody the way of death and wickedness—they are the fruits of the tree of the knowledge of good and evil, and they *turn us inward* and *make us sad*. They make us fit for the grey town. The opposing virtues are the fruits of the tree of life.[2] They turn us outward and orient us toward love of God and neighbor, expanding our very selves and freeing us for joy. They prepare us for the mountain country.

We turn now to the deadly sins and their opposing virtues in order to track this movement—one which turns us inward and leads to sadness and spiritual death, and the other which turns us outward and leads to joy and abundant life (see John 10:10).

The Deadly Sins

Lust. The problem with lust is not that it's sensual—the problem is that it focuses on a part and makes us think that part is all that matters. This is the core problem with pornography: not nakedness per se but, in Wojtyła's words, the tendency to evoke "in the recipient of this work . . . a conviction that *the sexual value is the only essential value of the person*, and that love is nothing else but experiencing or co-experiencing this value."[3]

Lust inclines us to devalue the other and bring a consumer mentality to the person, seeking to use them for the sake of a certain experience. It is love as desire gone awry, seeking to use another person to fill a need or desire in us. As we have seen, "sinful love" makes the experience primary (whether physical or emotional), over and against the objective good of the other person; the person becomes a mere means to this end. With lust, love deteriorates into use, the triumph of selfishness over self-giving love.

Chastity opposes lust by freeing our love from use. This virtue empowers us to love the other for their own sake and not merely for what they can do for us, enabling us to *personalize* our interaction with the other, elevating our reactions to the level of the person. For this reason, chastity is not a no but a great yes—a yes to the dignity of the person and to true love. In Wojtyła's words:

> Chastity is first and foremost a "yes," from which a "no" then proceeds. The underdevelopment of the virtue of chastity occurs when someone "does not keep up" with the affirmation of the value of the person, when he allows himself to be overpowered by the values of sex themselves which, upon seizing the will, form badly the whole relation to the person of the other sex. The essence of chastity lies precisely in

> "keeping up" with the value of the person in every situation and in "pulling up" to this value every reaction to the value of the "body and sex."

Chastity makes us "transparent," because it removes duplicity from our love.[4] While lust turns us inward in a self-centered way, chastity frees us to make a gift of ourselves in love.

Gluttony. Gluttony is a failure in temperance, regarding food and drink. Dining with other people is uniquely human, something often lost in the frenetic pace of modern life. Like lust, gluttony privileges the experience of food over people. It reverses the proper order of value.

In Catholic and Christian tradition, gluttony is about more than just quantity. For example, in *The Screwtape Letters*, Lewis speaks of "gluttony of delicacy,"[5] by which he means a preoccupation with having food prepared "just right," an excessive pickiness, as it were. In *The Screwtape Letters*, the person is unduly concerned with having things prepared *exactly* as she desires. Meanwhile, because the quantity is not large, she fails to recognize how enslaved she is to her palate.[6]

Temperance opposes gluttony by helping us utilize created goods for the glory of God in a manner befitting our human nature. While this virtue is typically thought of in terms of moderating our pursuit of bodily goods, we can also apply this virtue more broadly to anything that brings about emotional pleasure, such as social media.[7] Here, too, we need temperance to appreciate social media and make good use of it—and not become enslaved to it. In *Mere Christianity*, Lewis provides similar applications: "A man who makes his golf or his motor-bicycle the centre of his life, or a woman who devotes all her thoughts to clothes or bridge or her dog, is being just as 'intemperate' as someone who gets drunk every evening."[8]

These habits that ensnare us (whether food, drink, or social media) turn us inward and eventually make us sad. Temperance channels our desire for pleasure and created goods to their appropriate outlets—in the right manner, to the right degree, and at the right time, so that they don't take over our lives. Temperance frees us to turn outward and live the fully human life. It's kind of like dining at a Mexican restaurant—*if you fill up on chips and salsa, you'll miss out on the main course.* Temperance ensures that we get the most out of life by not getting overly ensnared by the various forms of "chips and salsa" that life has to offer.

Sloth. Sloth is sadness at the difficulty of the spiritual good.[9] Notice, *sadness* is part of its definition. This deadly sin captures the malaise that so often besets our culture today, creating a restlessness in the hearts of many, as life has become all too commonly a story with no plot.

Typical signs of sloth include *boredom*, *restlessness*, a deep sense of being *unfulfilled*, or *hatred of place*, where someone just can't stand where they are in life—a deep sense that real life is elsewhere. We can't remain in this sadness. If we can't find joy spiritually, we'll look for it physically. For this reason, sloth has stereotypical outlets, including *pleasure*—this could be food ("comfort food"), drugs, pornography, alcohol, or anything else to numb the pain. Another outlet for sloth is *entertainment*—this could be an obsession with the twenty-four-hour news cycle, a constant preoccupation with sports news, or the mindless scrolling of social media (anything to pass the time because we don't want to be alone with our thoughts). Sloth may also compel one to become a *workaholic*—this could be the sixty-plus-hour work week or the hyperfocus on fitness, worshipping at the altar of the mirror. In this last example, we see how a life of hyperbusyness can accompany sloth, as diligence here is masking an attempt to find meaning amid the hollowness of one's life.[10]

Sloth, then, is not laziness, pure and simple; it is a spiritual apathy or laziness regarding the highest things, which breeds a "carelessness of the heart" (*CCC* 2733) and a distaste for the things of God. The fact is, the more famished we are for spiritual food, the *less* drawn to it we become, as Augustine recounts his youth: "The more empty I was, the more I turned from it in revulsion."[11]

Spiritual diligence opposes the movement of sloth. To better enact spiritual diligence, we need the virtues of *discernment* and *magnanimity*. We cannot be spiritually diligent about everything—we cannot go after every apostolate or every devotional practice (just as one cannot do every exercise program at once). Discerning exactly what God wants us to pursue is key; otherwise, we just burn ourselves out and give up. *Magnanimity* means "greatness of soul" and is traditionally a part of courage.[12] It has to do with confidence and really going after things to the best of our ability and not selling ourselves short. Again, we cannot be magnanimous about everything at once. But if we discern where precisely to put our energies, we can go after our target with everything we have.

Sloth turns us inward because it makes us feel sorry for ourselves. Spiritual diligence—fueled by discernment and magnanimity—prepares us for life on mission, oriented outside ourselves for the glory of God and genuine love of neighbor. As we have seen, virtue expands our horizons and helps us become more. Vice—especially the deadly sins—turns us inward and make us lesser versions of ourselves.

Envy. Envy is sorrow at the good of another (or rejoicing in the misfortune of another).[13] Like sloth, envy has sadness as part of its definition. Traditionally, we distinguish envy from jealousy. The latter is *desiring the good of another* and can be morally neutral (depending on what one does with that desire).[14] For example, my desire to acquire the playing time my teammate is enjoying on a basketball team could lead me to reflect on the difference between our offseason work habits; it could lead me to imitate the good habits of my teammate with the hope of attaining the same good. However, jealousy may quickly turn to envy, which is never good. Envy plays a zero-sum game, because the other's good is my loss (and I rejoice at their misfortune).

Envy is diametrically opposed to love, and it destroys friendship. It leads to backbiting and gossip, and it preys on insecurity, as we attempt to increase our status by tearing others down. The virtue of charity (love) wills the good of the other and rejoices in their good; their joys and triumphs become our own—and their sorrows and defeats become our own as well. As St. Paul exhorts, "Rejoice with those who rejoice, weep with those who weep" (Rom 12:15). In friendship and genuine charity, we will the good of the other and become one heart and one mind.

Mercy also opposes envy. Mercy is love's response to suffering. It does not rejoice at the suffering of another—it pities their suffering and seeks to ameliorate it.[15]

Like all the deadly sins, envy turns us inward and makes us sad; it makes us preoccupied with ourselves, because we're constantly comparing ourselves with others. Charity and mercy turn us outward and free us for a life of joy and other-centered communion.

Pride. This deadly sin is a matter of radical self-absorption and self-centeredness. It is an attachment to our own ego, inclining us to defend it at all costs, much like the Big Ghost earlier. The vice here is not one of recognizing our own gifts and talents and the work we have put into developing them. Rather, pride is about trying to be our own ultimate end, to be "like God" but without him (see *CCC* 398). It is the refusal to orient our lives outward, toward God and neighbor. Pride is the ultimate collapse inward, losing ourselves in the abyss of our own ego.

Humility opposes pride. This virtue is often wildly misunderstood. Humility is about the *truth*, recognizing and accepting our strengths and limitations. It acknowledges God as the source of all our gifts, as well as taking note of how our family, friends, mentors, and coaches have helped us along the way. To deny our gifts is not humble, for that does not glorify God and his blessings, nor does it accurately capture the truth about ourselves.

As Lewis articulates so well, humility is about taking our eyes off ourselves and turning outward in love of God and neighbor. In the words of the fictional demon in *The Screwtape Letters*: "By this virtue [humility], as by all the others, our Enemy [God] wants to turn the man's attention away from self to Him, and to the man's neighbors." This self-forgetfulness is the "true end of humility," the virtue that facilitates authentic love.[16]

The irony of being preoccupied with our faults and weaknesses is that it turns our mind back upon ourselves—thereby undermining genuine humility. For this reason, the demon in *The Screwtape Letters* concludes, "Even of his sins the Enemy [God] does not want him to think too much: once they are repented, the sooner the man turns his attention outward, the better the Enemy is pleased."[17] Although we must take sin seriously, once we've repented of it—and as Catholics, once we have brought it to the Sacrament of Reconciliation—we have to let it go. There is a sense in which taking our own sins too seriously (as if they were beyond the reach of God's mercy and forgiveness) is at root taking *ourselves* too seriously. Our sins are never too big for God.

The name *Satan* in Hebrew means "to accuse." In temptation, Satan is our buddy, coaxing us into sin. But after we fall, he becomes the *accuser*, seeking to douse us in shame (see Zechariah 3:1-5).[18] Consequently, obsessing over our sin and brokenness plays directly into his hand—it is exactly what he wants. We must ask ourselves, what is the source of our sadness when we have sinned? Are we sad because we have offended the one whom we love? Or are we sad in part because we are witnessing the *fracturing of the idealized picture we have of ourselves*? In other words, is our sadness at root due to pride?

Humility lies in embracing the full truth about ourselves and overcoming our impulse toward self-absorption (i.e., thinking less *about* ourselves). These two aspects of humility lead to a third: namely, *deliberately looking for the good in others.*[19] In this way, humility counteracts not only pride but envy as well.

Pride quintessentially turns us inward, making us isolated and sad, very much at home in the grey town of *The Great Divorce*. Humility is *the* virtue that facilitates our outward turn toward God and neighbor. It disposes us toward the fullness of reality, opening us to receive the *gift* of reality. This is the key virtue that enables one to journey into the mountain country, because it paves the way for love.

Anger. The deadly sin of anger (or wrath) can occur when our reactions are disproportionate, where we have dramatic outbursts. Meekness moderates our anger. It is, in effect, *temperance applied to anger*, so that our feelings of anger do not derail us from pursuing the good. Meekness is not weakness; it takes great strength to maintain self-control.

More typically, however, anger concerns the bitter rancor of long-held resentments that poison our relationships and resist forgiveness. In addition to meekness, the virtue of forgiveness heals the wounds of long-held grudges and resentment.

Importantly, forgiveness does not always entail reconciliation; it is not necessarily a matter of forgetting the past or no longer having strong feelings about it. Forgiveness at its core is about *surrendering the debt*—the debt another owes us for having wronged us. While surrendering this debt is a tremendous gift to the other person, it is also a powerful moment of liberation for us. Forgiveness frees our hearts from the prison of the past. It frees us to turn outward in the present moment and not remain stuck in the past.

Anger tends to turn us inward, causing us to stew over how others have wronged us. While it can lead to positive action (say, if injustice moves us to do good), very often anger locks us up within ourselves, as we brood over grievances wrought against us. We quickly assume the part of the victim (which is sometimes, no doubt, truly the case). But often, conflict and tension build over time, usually with more than one person at fault. While we may have been truly wronged, stewing over it prevents us from taking responsibility and seeking forgiveness for the part we may have contributed to the conflict. As such, it becomes a festering poison within our hearts and keeps us imprisoned in the past.

Conversely, meekness and forgiveness (and humility!) enable us to see things from the other's point of view, perhaps bringing us to realize that our version of the story—while potentially and even largely accurate—may not be the whole picture. Forgiveness allows us to stop projecting the past upon the present and enables us to move forward in our relationships. It helps us move beyond the continuous defense of our egos—our rights and our desire for retaliation for past grievances.

Avarice. Avarice or greed is a perennial temptation for human beings, especially today. The temptation is strong because of the security money provides. At times past, one could only utilize so much natural wealth, such as land, for example. But there is something artificial and infinite about an electronic bank account, with no real "limit" to our desire or perceived need. On the one hand, the Church has always maintained the right to private property, as befitting human freedom and as an appropriate safeguard for the autonomy and integrity of the family (i.e., making a profit is not wrong).[20] However, on the other hand, we are called to *use* our private property with an eye toward the common good.[21] Ultimately, the right to private property must be subordinated to another principle, the *universal destination of all goods* (see *CCC* 2403–2404), which means that the goods of the earth are destined for the entire human family.[22]

We are stewards of our lives, not owners. This should lead us to be generous with our means in whatever way we can.[23] The virtue of generosity clearly opposes avarice and turns us outward, helping us realize that *gift* is at the heart of everything. Our lives are gift, and we are called to make a gift of our lives in return, to God and neighbor.

Sorrow. Some parts of the Christian tradition see sorrow as a deadly sin.[24] Sorrow in this sense is not the ordinary emotion of sadness or the condition of clinical depression. What is meant here is an *irrational sadness that loses sight of eternity.* In Brant Pitre's words, "If a spirit of sadness comes over us that leads us to stop praying, then it is definitely the sinful kind."[25]

The virtue of patience opposes this movement of sorrow because patience enables us to bear trials with peace of mind, serenity, and even a deep-seated joy. Our Lord calls us not to be "anxious" four times in the Sermon on the Mount (see Matthew 6:25–34). Though there are different forms of anxiety, in my experience, the power of Jesus's exhortation lies in the fact that *anxiety can paralyze our ability to love and be present to those around us.* When I have been overwhelmed by my own concerns and worries, even if I am physically in the same room, I'm not emotionally available. Patience enables us to continue to be other-centered and emotionally present, even when things are not going our way—even when our lives turn in directions we never envisioned.

Hope also opposes sorrow. By this virtue, we long for our eternal union with God and trust that he will give us what we need to make it to our final end. Hope is not mere optimism that things will get better or work out. The heart of hope runs deeper. Hope bears a deep sense that (1) our ultimate home is not in this life; and (2) despite appearances to the contrary, *God is at work.* Despite the way things seem, what Joseph says to his brothers is perennially true: "As for you, you meant evil against me; but God meant it for good, to bring it about that many people should be kept alive, as they are today" (Gn 50:20).

Hope aims at the *difficult* but *possible* good. It always entails some fear, since "hope" means we're not there yet. If we think of salvation, for example, as *not difficult*—that we don't really need to repent or change—then we fall into *presumption*. But if we think of salvation as *not possible* (as if our sins are too big for God), then we fall into *despair*.

So, is it okay to hope for earthly things—that we get this job, or that our children receive this or that opportunity? The answer is yes, but with an important qualification. As difficult as it is to say, our prayer needs to be something like the following: "Lord, please grant us this earthly good, *as long as it's conducive to our reaching our final end in you*." We must strive to say with sincerity, "If this earthly good would prevent me or my loved ones from reaching our final end in you, *then we don't want it*." With great faith, we want to be able to say: "I choose you, Lord, the giver of all gifts, over the gifts themselves."

Patience and hope are galvanized by the perspective of eternity. In the words of St. John Cassian, a contemporary of St. Augustine: "We shall be able to overcome every kind of sadness . . . when we are ever rejoicing at the sight of things eternal."[26]

2 Trees—one leading to death, one leading to life [27]

(fruits of the tree of the knowledge of good and evil)	*(fruits of the tree of life)*
lust	chastity
gluttony	temperance
sloth	spiritual diligence
envy	charity/mercy
pride	humility
anger	meekness/forgiveness
avarice	generosity
sorrow	patience/hope

Which Tree Do We Want?

Sin turns us inward and makes us sad. It locks us into a world absorbed by our own egos and cut off from authentic love and communion—the very essence of the grey town.

Virtue turns us outward and frees us for love of God and neighbor. It frees us to let go of ourselves and make a gift of our lives in love. The true meaning of our lives is revealed in Jesus Christ. In imitation of him, we are called to *communion through total self-gift*. Virtue makes this possible, for it is self-mastery that makes possible self-gift.[28] Conversely, enslavement to sin is enslavement to our own egos. This is the inward turn, the path of bitter nihilism, the choice of nothingness.

One path leads to life and one to death. But this death is not imposed from without. As we have seen in *The Great Divorce*, this death is the slow withering away of our souls, of our very selves. As authentic love decreases, we decrease as well. This is why heaven and hell are *retrospective*. "Heaven" is not just a place we're going, and "hell" not just a place we're trying to avoid. "Both processes begin even before death," writes Lewis. We are either growing in one direction or the other, either toward the fullness of reality, love, and selflessness—or toward the self-centered worship of our own egos and the nihilistic nothingness that follows: "And that is why, at the end of all things, when the sun rises here [in the mountain country] and the twilight turns to blackness down there [in the grey town], the Blessed will say 'We have never lived anywhere except Heaven,' and the Lost, 'We were always in Hell.'"[29]

The choice of life or death is ever before us, existing always in the present moment, where time and eternity intersect. *God* or *nothingness*—we must decide.

"Choose life," Moses exhorts (Dt 30:19). In Jesus's words: "I came that they may have life, and have it abundantly" (Jn 10:10). To stake our lives on Jesus is to choose life. "God is love" (1 Jn 4:8), and Jesus is the answer to the deepest yearning of the human heart. As St. John Paul II was so fond of repeating, *Jesus Christ is the answer to the question that is every human life*:

> It is Jesus in fact that you seek when you dream of happiness; he is waiting for you when nothing else you find satisfies you; he is the beauty to which you are so attracted; it is he who provokes you with that thirst for fullness that will not let you settle for compromise; it is he who urges you to shed the masks of a false life; it is he who reads in your hearts your most genuine choices, the choices that others try to stifle. It is Jesus who stirs in you the desire to do something great with your lives, the will to follow an ideal, the refusal to allow yourselves to be grounded down by mediocrity, the courage to commit yourselves humbly and patiently to improving yourselves and society, making the world more human and more fraternal.[30]

Jesus loves us just as we are, but too much to leave us that way. He simultaneously offers unconditional mercy *and* a call to greatness. He sees something in us that we too often fail to see in ourselves. Let us trust him and journey with him to the mountain country, further up and further in.[31] For the infinity of God—his beauty and his love—is ageless and endless. We have everything to gain and nothing to lose, save the "masks of a false life." Let us take the journey into the real, into the inexhaustible love of the Father, ever ancient and ever new.

After all, what else are we waiting for?

ELEVEN

Preparing for the Bridegroom

Death and taxes are our colloquial certainties. No one is getting out of here alive, at least not in our earthly bodies. Sickness and death bring us face-to-face with our own contingency, our utter lack of control—despite the ways in which our advancing technology might deceive us into thinking otherwise.

What does it mean to have a "happy" and "holy" death? How would we like our end to be when it's time? The key, it seems, is to have prepared along the way.

Witold Pilecki, a devout Catholic and Polish war hero, embodies this well. His story almost defies imagination. Celebrated for his role in the "Miracle on the Vistuła," the battle the Poles won in 1920 against the rising Soviet communism, he then devised an unbelievably daring plan during World War II. He would get himself caught by the Gestapo and taken to Auschwitz; there, he would gather intelligence and lead a prisoner revolt—which, if supported by an Allied attack, would take over the camp. Proceeding with his plan, he found himself in Auschwitz and began collecting intelligence and building up prisoner morale. Frustrated with the delay of the Allies, he eventually escaped and traveled to Warsaw to make his case in person for an Allied attack. His reports on the atrocities at the camp seemed exaggerated, and the hoped-for attack never came.

Toward the end of the war, Pilecki began gathering intelligence on Communist activities in Poland, in hopes of preventing a Communist takeover after the war. Shortly after the war ended, the Communists put Pilecki to death on trumped-up charges. This Polish war hero did not even receive a burial. This was the environment in which the young Fr. Karol Wojtyła began his priestly ministry in Communist Poland.[1]

Shortly before being sentenced to death, Pilecki told the Communist court: "I tried to live my life in such a fashion so that in my last hour, I would be happy rather than fearful" (in some translations: "that . . . I would feel *joy* rather than *fear*").[2] The way we go out will have everything to do with how we have *lived*. Those who have long prepared for death—by living the way they intended to live—will face death with greater peace, even perhaps with the joy and serenity of Pilecki, knowing that this life is not the end.

Facing the Last Enemy—Death Itself

Catholics have traditionally reflected upon the four last things before bed each night: *death*, *judgment*, *heaven*, and *hell*. Every Ash Wednesday, we hear the words, "You are dust, and to dust you shall return" (Gn 3:19), reminding us of our mortality. We also hear the prophet Joel's call to repentance: "Return to me with all your heart, with fasting, with weeping, and with mourning; and tear your hearts and not your garments" (Jl 2:12–13).

We know from Scripture that there is a mysterious connection between sin and human death (see *CCC* 1008), as humankind forfeited the gift of grace that would have preserved our integrity (see *CCC* 404–405). This is why Jesus defeats the "last enemy," death itself (1 Cor 15:26).

All humanity is implicated in the fall of Adam, as our covenant representative; so, too, all can enter into Christ's victory (see Romans 5:19, 6:3–4, and *CCC* 404). What is new when it comes to death for a Christian is that the Christian has already died in Christ—and already now shares in his Resurrection (see *CCC* 1010). The whole sacramental economy of faith is an entrance into Christ's death and Resurrection. Especially in the Eucharist, our reception of Christ's risen body, we have tangible hope of our victory over the grave: "Our participation in the

Eucharist already gives us a foretaste of Christ's transfiguration of our bodies" (*CCC* 1000). In St. Irenaeus's words, writing in AD 180: "Our bodies which partake of the Eucharist are no longer corruptible, but possess the hope of resurrection" (cited in *CCC* 1000).[3]

The Coming of Christ

The Greek word *parousia* is typically understood with reference to Christ's Second Coming, as we profess in the Creed ("he will come again to judge the living and the dead"). However, the coming of Christ has multiple layers of meaning in Sacred Scripture.

First, the "coming" of the Lord in the Old Testament usually refers not to the end of the space-time universe, but to his coming *in* history, typically against a power that is oppressing his people. The prophets use cataclysmic language (e.g., stars falling, sun darkening) to describe this coming of God in history, as Isaiah does, for example, in describing the downfall of Babylon at the hands of the Medo-Persians, an event that takes place in 539 BC (see Isaiah 13:1, 9–10, 17). Consequently, when Jesus uses this same language, he is not referring only (or primarily) to the end of all things (e.g., Mt 24:29)—and that's why he can say that such events will happen "within a generation" (Mt 24:34). What Jesus is referring to is in part the fall of the Temple in AD 70, which manifests the definitive giving way of the Old Covenant and the ushering in of the New (see *CCC* 586).[4]

Second, the Greek word *parousia* literally means "presence."[5] So, every Eucharist—the real presence of Christ—is truly Christ's *parousia* (see *CCC* 1373–1381, 1402–1405). Every Eucharist is a *coming* of Christ among us.

Third, Jesus comes for each one of us at the time of our death. We must prepare and be watchful, like the wise virgins of Matthew 25: "Watch therefore, for you know neither the day nor the hour" (v. 13). The foolish virgins do not have oil for their lamps and are asleep (see Matthew 25:3–5). They are not ready to meet the Bridegroom, Jesus Christ.

As mentioned earlier, in *The Jeweler's Shop*, Adam shows Anna the "wise virgins," who "are dressed according to the climate and customs of our country."[6] That is, they look just like everyone else; their difference is interior. The foolish virgins are asleep; they have fallen into a spiritual stupor—they have lost their way.

Upon our death, we will receive the judgment of Christ, and our destiny will be manifest (see *CCC* 1021 and Hebrews 9:27).[7] While our eternal fate will be set at this point, in the Last Judgment at the end of time (the Second Coming), we will see the full truth of our relationship to Christ, to its furthest rippling throughout the entirety of history.[8] "In the presence of Christ, who is Truth itself, the truth of each man's relationship with God will be laid bare. The Last Judgment will reveal *even to its furthest consequences* the good each person has done or failed to do during his earthly life" (*CCC* 1039, emphasis added). Only then will we see the total meaning of our lives, as everything comes to light.

Thus, we can distinguish four separate "comings" of Christ—four dimensions of his *parousia*:

- *historical* (AD 70): destruction of the Temple and the definitive giving way of the Old Covenant and ushering in of the New
- *liturgical*: in the Holy Eucharist
- *personal*: at the time of our death
- *eschatological*: Second Coming at the end of time (the Last Judgment)

How Can We Be Ready?

As we saw earlier, for Anna to avoid becoming a foolish virgin—to avoid falling asleep—she must awaken herself to what matters most. She must resist the temptation to aimlessly drift along in life, without purpose or intentionality. In the busyness of the day-to-day, it is so easy to lose sight of the true target of our lives.

Key spiritual practices can make all the difference, especially if we are consistent. For starters, each night, we should take a few minutes to run through our day and do a personal examination, asking ourselves questions such as:

- What are we thankful for?
- What are we worried about that we need to surrender to the Lord?
- What are we sorry for, and where do we sense the Lord prodding us to grow? What in our life needs to be removed, and what should be added?

Doing this consistently keeps us in touch with the Holy Spirit. It keeps us from running on autopilot, wandering through life and falling asleep spiritually, as it were. It keeps us anchored in what matters most and provides a constant check when things get off track. Doing this each night—placing ourselves before the truth and mercy of God—becomes a dress rehearsal for the final time we go to bed and don't wake up. Each nightly examination is a preparation for our final judgment. We do not know when the Lord will call us home. But like Pilecki, by living intentionally and preparing along the way, we can face our end with joy rather than fear.

Another powerful practice is to envision ourselves upon our deathbed and evaluate our life from that standpoint. What does my current life look like from the viewpoint of my deathbed self? What does the hundred-year-old version of myself think of how I am living now? How does that person evaluate my current concerns and priorities? Am I living in such a way that would make the deathbed version of myself proud?

This perspective gives us a long view that we easily lose sight of in the hustle and bustle of daily life. This long-range view of our lives keeps our hearts attuned to what matters most.

A third crucial practice is mental prayer, by which I simply mean "listening" prayer. My favorite place for mental prayer is before the Blessed Sacrament, but that is not always possible. It can be done anywhere, often with Scripture or some spiritual reading as an aid; but the key is that it is not a study session—it's a time for *listening* to the voice of God. If this is new to you, begin with five minutes; eventually work up to ten or fifteen (maybe even twenty or thirty) minutes. At first, this will be difficult; it will be hard to sit still, and the silence can be overwhelming. If you are using Scripture or some spiritual reading, be sure to read no more than a paragraph. You are asking the Lord to speak to you through these words; the reading is a prompt, a beginning point, not the end.

Use this time to ask the Lord personal questions, similar to the nightly examination:

- How are you calling me, Lord?
- What in my life needs to change?
- How are you working deep within me to heal me and make me whole? Help me to understand—in your presence and by your grace—who I truly am and who you are calling me to be.
- How is my past still living on in and (negatively) affecting my present?

In the depths of prayer, God reveals to us who he is *and* who we truly are.

It is difficult to continue for very long in serious sin when we engage in this kind of prayer. The silence is just too loud. Either we will stop praying in this way or the particular sin we're struggling with will start to lose some of its power over us. Unfortunately, it *is* possible to engage in vocal prayer—even daily Mass—and live a double life. For this reason, mental prayer, where we speak heart-to-heart with the Lord, is truly transformative. If we are consistent here, our lives will never be the same.

In my experience, this type of prayer (along with a strong sacramental life) fosters immense *clarity* and *strength*. I have found that, when I pray this way consistently, whatever the Lord is calling me to tends to come into sharper and sharper focus. What often begins as a gentle knock on the heart gets unmistakably louder and clearer with time. Consistently praying in this way has also brought great strength, often empowering me to do what I couldn't have imagined doing only a few months prior (e.g., making a hard decision or having a hard conversation).

In addition to clarity and strength, this form of prayer has brought deep *healing* in my life. It has brought me to see depths within myself in a new and healing light, as the journey of conversion runs ever deeper. It has enabled me to take tremendous strides in forgiveness—both in seeking forgiveness from others and in forgiving those who have hurt me. Indeed, Jesus makes all things new. In mental prayer especially, we begin to take on his mind and his heart, to see ourselves as he sees us and to see others as he sees them. As the sun changes our complexion, so, too, sitting in the holy presence of Jesus (especially before the Blessed Sacrament) conforms us to his image and likeness. It helps us to look upon others with love and mercy, and to be more attentive to the part we have played in wounding various relationships.

This form of prayer has also been critical for me in coming to accept the suffering that the Lord has allowed me or my family to undergo. As we said earlier, this deep acceptance of the circumstances of our lives is a way of "forgiving" God. Even more, this deep acceptance becomes a source of interior healing—not because we are fond of the suffering, but because we come to see that God was never absent and that an unseen plan was always mysteriously unfolding, even in our suffering. Our anger toward the people and circumstances of our past begins to subside, as we more thoroughly entrust our lives to the loving (and mysterious) hands of divine providence. "Forgiving" God means accepting and embracing his plan for our lives, in all its twists and turns. He didn't wrong us; but we have to work through our deep feelings that he has done so with brutal honesty. Mental prayer (along with counseling and spiritual direction) is one of the most significant ways we can begin this healing process.

In sum, three life-changing practices that enable us to live with intentionality and purpose and prepare for the coming of the Bridegroom are:

- nightly examination
- deathbed meditation (what does the deathbed version of myself think of how I am living?)
- mental prayer (listening prayer)

Perhaps very few of us will be truly ready for death, since we have so little experience with it, especially in the modern context. But if we are daily growing with the Lord, daily entering ever more fully into Christ and his victory over sin and death, we need not fear coming into the light. We will come before the heart of the Father, before the most merciful Jesus. If we are living each day as if it could be the end, we have nothing to fear. But if we "sleep" through life, with aimlessness and lack of purpose, the Lord's coming for us will be something we do not expect, something for which we are not prepared.

Jesus makes all things new and brings all things to light. We give the Evil One the upper hand when we suppress things in the dark. Heartfelt, listening prayer and examining our lives every day brings our "junk" to light. The Lord is not afraid of our sin, nor is he disgusted by it. It is we who cannot stand ourselves. He *delights* in us. Prayer helps us embrace this truth. He is the Divine Physician, seeking to make us whole, putting the fragments of our life back together.

The only real tragedy in life is to close ourselves off from his love, in this life and the next. "God desires all men to be saved" (1 Tm 2:4). For this reason, "The Church prays that no one should be lost" (*CCC* 1058). As Lewis put it earlier, there are only two kinds of people: those who say to God, "Thy will be done," and those to whom God says, "*Thy* will be done."[9]

If we come into the light, the light of Christ will overcome the darkness (see John 1:4). We need only bring our whole selves, our deepest selves, into his healing gaze. To be fully healed, we must come before him as we truly are—wounded and broken: "Behold, I stand at the door and knock; if any one hears my voice and opens the door, I will come into him and eat with him, and he with me" (Rv 3:20).

The door of our hearts can only be locked from the inside. The moment we open fully to the Lord "contains all moments,"[10] as the angel told the man with the lizard. May we not hold anything back and instead enjoy the endless beauty of the mountain country, the deepest yearning of the human heart. Submitting to God's truth and allowing our attachments to die and be raised anew is precisely how we find the deepest and most exalted version of ourselves. We will become as radiant as the mountain country and discover it as our true and final home, the ultimate object of our hope and longing.

Life with the Bridegroom

So, will we be bored in heaven? Not if we're thinking sacramentally and typologically. Not if we're thinking in step with Lewis—that heaven is *more real* than this life, and far more real than hell.

The emptiness of hell is the self-withering of self-centeredness. As we collapse in on the black hole of our own egos—and get to the point where we cannot see beyond ourselves, our self-importance and self-interest—we find ourselves diminished, shriveling up into nothingness. We have closed our fists and can no longer receive the gift of reality, the gift of another in love. Closed off from love, we wither, unable to enter into true communion with one another. Not with God, and not with anyone else, as is manifest in the loneliness and isolation of the grey town.

The converse is also true. Love and humility expand our horizons. They open our hands to receive reality as gift, and to receive the other as gift—and to give ourselves away in total self-giving love. This is the great paradox of the mountain country and Christian life: *In giving, we receive.* In loving and giving ourselves away in love, we do not lose ourselves but paradoxically find ourselves enhanced and elevated beyond anything we could have imagined.

This love, however, requires the Cross. This love entails some pain, the pain of letting go of ourselves, and the risk of losing ourselves. What is lost, however, is the self-centered part of us, the part unable and unwilling to enter the exchange of love.

The Great Divorce charts this pain as the journey into the mountain country. It hurts because we are not accustomed to the fullness of reality; *we* are not enough to endure the journey. Love hurts because our fallen nature does not love easily or spontaneously. But each step into the mountain country—each step with the grace of Christ—makes the next step a little more adept, a little easier, as *we* become more. The journey transforms us. Life is a pilgrimage back to the heart of the Father. Both the end and the journey are crucial, because the journey changes us, making us fit to enjoy the Bridegroom for all eternity.

We find our true selves in relation to one another. In relationship, we find ourselves and our healing. To journey into the mountain country is to enter the fullness of communion—the fullness of joy, intimacy, understanding, and total self-giving love. This is heaven. This is reality. This is joy.

May we prefer nothing whatever to joy, nothing whatever to Christ.

Our eternal fate hinges on this choice, and we make our choice in the present moment. *We* decide our eternal fate—it is never imposed upon us from the outside.

Joy, Love, Reality—God; or self?

Joy, Love, Reality—God; or *nothing*?

That is the question, and only we can decide the answer.

Notes

Introduction

1. C. S. Lewis, *Mere Christianity* (HarperCollins, 2001), 136–37.

2. *The Confessions: Saint Augustine of Hippo*, trans. Maria Boulding, ed. David Vincent Meconi (Ignatius, 2012), 9.10 at pp. 250–53.

3. *Confessions* 9.10 at p. 251.

4. *Confessions* 7.12 and 7.15 at pp. 182 and 184.

5. See Joseph Owens, *An Elementary Christian Metaphysics* (Center for Thomistic Studies, 1985), 111–24.

6. *Confessions* 7.11 at p. 181.

1. Are There Really *Intellectual* Sins?

1. See bk. VI in *Aristotle: Nicomachean Ethics*, trans. Terence Irwin, 2nd ed. (Hackett, 1999), 86–98. For Aristotle, the intellectual virtues fall into two categories, speculative (those ordered toward *knowing*) and practical (those ordered toward *doing* or *making*). Among the practical intellectual virtues, Aristotle places prudence (the intellectual virtue by which we make moral decisions—hence "doing") and art (which is reason applied to what is made—referring to the work of any craftsman, not just fine arts, hence "making"). The intellectual virtues ordered toward knowing are wisdom, understanding, and science. Understanding is about first principles, and science is about reasoning discursively from first principles. Wisdom combines understanding and science and places them in the context of grasping the most ultimate causes; that is, wisdom entails knowing the deepest *why* we can come to. All these virtues perfect the intellectual capacities rooted in our human nature and constitute for Aristotle an important dimension of the virtuous life (and therefore, our pursuit of happiness). These "virtues of thought" (which perfect the intellect in terms of knowing, doing, and making) must be accompanied by "virtues of character" (principally temperance, courage, and justice), which perfect our human nature with respect to the will and our emotional life. See bk II in *Aristotle: Nicomachean Ethics*, 18–29.

2. See Andrew Swafford, *Lunatic, Liar, or Lord: Unveiling the Truth of Catholicism with C. S. Lewis's "Mere Christianity"* (Ave Maria Press, 2025), 22–24.

3. See C. S. Lewis, *The Great Divorce* (HarperCollins, 1946), 33–44.

4. Lewis, *Great Divorce*, 35.

5. See Lewis, *Great Divorce*, 34–36.

6. Lewis, *Great Divorce*, 36, emphasis added.

7. Lewis, *Great Divorce*, 34, emphasis added.

8. Lewis, *Great Divorce*, 36.

9. Lewis, *Great Divorce*, 36, 37, emphasis added.

10. C. S. Lewis, *The Screwtape Letters* (Harper San Francisco, 2001), 50.

11. Lewis, *Screwtape Letters*, 49.

12. Lewis, *Great Divorce*, 38.

13. Lewis, *Great Divorce*, 39.

14. Lewis, *Great Divorce*, 39, 40.

15. Lewis, *Great Divorce*, 40, emphasis in original.

16. Lewis, *Great Divorce*, 40 (emphasis added), 41.

17. Overcoming this fact-value divide is exactly the point of C. S. Lewis's *Abolition of Man*. See *The Abolition of Man: or Reflections on Education with Special Reference to the Teaching of English in the Upper Forms of Schools* (Macmillan Publishing, 1965), 39–63.

18. Pope Benedict XVI coined this phrase shortly before being elected pope in 2005 and used it throughout his pontificate. See Gediminas T. Jankunas, *The Dictatorship of Relativism: Pope Benedict XVI's Response* (Alba House, 2011).

19. In truth, the view we are describing is known as "scientism" (the view that all knowledge comes through the scientific method—and that any claim to knowledge outside the scientific method is merely subjective opinion). This is actually a *philosophical* claim (about the nature and limits of human knowledge), not a scientific one—as the claim of scientism itself cannot be verified by the scientific method. Respect for science is something very much at home in the Catholic tradition. But Catholics are rightly leery of philosophical attempts to smuggle materialistic-atheistic philosophy under the guise of science, recognizing that this is not science but bad philosophy masquerading as science.

20. See Regensburg Address, September 12, 2006, https://www.vatican.va/content/benedict-xvi/en/speeches/2006/september/documents/hf_ben-xvi_spe_20060912_university-regensburg.html.

21. Lewis, *Great Divorce*, 42.

22. Lewis, *Great Divorce*, 43–44.

2. Faith and the Heart

1. Robert George (@McCormickProf. 2020): "1/ I sometimes ask students what their position on slavery would have been had they been white and living in the South before abolition. Guess what? They all would have been abolitionists! They all would have bravely spoken out against slavery, and worked tirelessly against it.

"2/ Of course, this is nonsense. Only the tiniest fraction of them, or of any of us, would have spoken up against slavery or lifted a finger to free the slaves. Most of them—and us—would have gone along. Many would have supported the slave system and happily benefited from it.

"3/ So I respond by saying that I will credit their claims if they can show evidence of the following: that in leading their lives today they have stood up for the rights of unpopular victims of injustice whose very humanity is denied, and where they have done so knowing:

"4/ (1) that it would make them unpopular with their peers, (2) that they would be loathed and ridiculed by powerful, influential individuals and institutions in our society; (3) that they would be abandoned by many of their friends, (4) that they would be called nasty names, and

"5/ (5) that they would risk being denied valuable professional opportunities as a result of their moral witness. In short, my challenge is to show where they have at risk to themselves and their futures stood up for a cause that is unpopular in elite sectors of our culture today." (Twitter (now X), July 1, 2020, 10:23 p.m., https://x.com/McCormickProf/status/1278529694355292161)

2. See Pope Francis, Angelus Address, January 29, 2023, https://www.vatican.va/content/francesco/en/angelus/2023/documents/20230129-angelus.html.

3. See *CCC* 880–896.

4. Lewis points to this in *The Screwtape Letters*, suggesting that the demonic world encourages our confusion with regard to what are truly the most pressing problems of our time: "We [the demonic tempters] direct the fashionable outcry of each generation against those vices of which it is least in danger and fix its approval on the virtues nearest to that vice which we are trying to make endemic. The game is to have them all running about with fire extinguishers whenever there is a flood. . . . Thus we make it fashionable to expose the dangers of enthusiasm at the very moment when they are all really becoming worldly and lukewarm" (137–38).

5. See *Summa Contra Gentiles*: "In this faith [Christianity] there are truths preached that surpass every human intellect; the pleasures of the flesh are curbed; it is taught that the things of the world should be spurned. Now, for the minds of mortal men to assent to these things is the greatest of miracles" (*Saint Thomas Aquinas: Summa Contra Gentiles, Book One: God*, trans. Anton C. Pegis [University of Notre Dame Press, 1975], bk. 1, ch. 6, at p. 72).

6. Lewis, *Mere Christianity*, 141.

7. Marcellino D'Ambrosio and Andrew Swafford, *What We Believe: The Beauty of the Catholic Faith* (Ascension, 2022), 40–41.

8. Joseph Ratzinger, *Introduction to Christianity*, trans. J. R. Foster (Ignatius Press, 1990), 39–40.

9. Swafford, *Lunatic, Liar, or Lord*, 111–13.

10. Of course, marketing can have a positive and even Christian dimension—by making people aware of something that can help them and serve their authentic human flourishing.

11. Lewis suggests something similar in *Abolition of Man* when he says, "The head rules the belly through the chest" (34). If we are emotionally

inclined toward God but have serious intellectual blocks, it is unlikely that emotion alone can sustain our journey of faith. If we are intellectually convinced but our devotion and piety remain emotionally unconnected to the Lord, the faith easily becomes an idea that we assent to but not something that truly becomes central to our lives (and the faith as an abstract idea in this sense can accompany much grave sin). But in my experience (personally and walking with many others, including numerous college students), fostering intellectual conviction *and* our affective connection to the Lord nurtures a strong and sustainable faith life over the long haul. This path is also very powerful for growth in the spiritual life and overcoming sin.

12. In Scripture, "heart" (*leb* and *kardia* in Hebrew and Greek, respectively) refers not merely to emotion or sentiment but to the inner core of the person, encompassing all three aspects described above (intellect, will, emotion). This more profound meaning of "heart" lies behind the Bible's call to love the Lord our God with all our "heart" and the promise of a new "heart" through the gift of the Spirit (see Deuteronomy 6:4–5; Mark 12:29–30; Ezekiel 36:26; Jeremiah 31:33; and Romans 5:5).

13. James Hitchcock, *History of the Catholic Church: From the Apostolic Age to the Third Millenium* (Ignatius, 2012), 266–84.

14. For example: "Agnosticism can sometimes include a certain search for God, but it can equally express indifferentism, a flight from the ultimate question of existence, and a sluggish moral conscience. Agnosticism is all too often equivalent to practical atheism" (*CCC* 2128).

15. The *Catechism* describes prayer as a battle, sometimes with ourselves, as it requires a serious and intentional effort "against ourselves and against the wiles of the tempter who does all he can to turn man away from prayer, away from union with God" (2725). The vitality of our spiritual lives is inextricably intertwined with prayer: "We pray as we live, because we live as we pray. If we do not want to act habitually according to the Spirit of Christ, neither can we pray habitually in his name. The 'spiritual battle' of the Christian's new life is inseparable from the battle of prayer" (*CCC* 2725).

16. The *Catechism* twice draws attention to a French word, *théologal*, to capture the heart of Christian life (2607, 2803). The French Catholic theological tradition is careful to distinguish this word from a similar French word, *théologique*. The latter refers to theological *knowledge*, the fruit of theological study. The former refers to theological *life*, the dynamic life animated by the theological virtues of faith, hope, and charity. *Théologal* life is fundamentally a participation in God's life—in his revelation to us (through faith) and in his love poured into our hearts through the Holy Spirit (through hope and love; see Romans 5:5). The path of Jesus and his own prayer in his humanity is the *théologal* path (see *CCC* 2607). This gives rise to our filial boldness in Christ (*parrhesia* in the Greek New Testament; see Hebrews 4:16; *CCC* 2599, 2610), as we enter into and embrace our status as children of the Father in the

Son. Christian life is a dynamic participation in the life of the Son, including the newfound relation we have through him in prayer. "In the Holy Spirit, Christian prayer is a communion of love with the Father, not only through Christ but also *in him*" (*CCC* 2615, emphasis added). See Romanus Cessario, *Christian Faith and the Theological Life* (Catholic University of America Press, 1996), 1–2. St. John Paul II draws attention to this French word (*théologal*) in his catechesis on the theology of the body (see TOB 127:1–3, cited in John Paul II, *Man and Woman He Created Them: A Theology of the Body*, trans. Michael Waldstein [Pauline Books and Media, 2006], 642–43).

17. Karol Wojtyła, *Love and Responsibility*, trans. Grzegorz Ignatik (Pauline Books and Media, 2013), 121.

3. The Relentless Grip of One's Ego

1. Lewis, *Great Divorce*, 25–31.
2. Lewis, *Great Divorce*, 27, emphasis added.
3. Lewis, *Great Divorce*, 27–28.
4. Lewis, *Great Divorce*, 28.
5. Lewis, *Great Divorce*, 29, emphasis added.
6. Lewis, *Great Divorce*, 29.
7. Lewis, *Great Divorce*, 29–30.
8. Lewis, *Great Divorce*, 31, emphasis added.
9. See Lewis, *Great Divorce*, 30.
10. Robert D. Enright, *Forgiveness Is a Choice: A Step-by-Step Process for Resolving Anger and Restoring Hope* (American Psychological Association, 2001), 49.
11. See Joseph Grenny, Kerry Patterson, Ron McMillan, Al Switzler, and Emily Gregory, *Crucial Conversations: Tools for Talking When Stakes Are High*, 3rd ed. (McGraw Hill, 2022), 78–80.
12. Grenny et al., *Crucial Conversations*, 82, 87.
13. Enright, *Forgiveness Is a Choice*, 89, emphasis added.

4. Humility and Ambition—What's a Christian to Do?

1. Lewis, *Great Divorce*, 82–87.
2. Lewis, *Great Divorce*, 83, emphasis in original.
3. Lewis, *Great Divorce*, 84.
4. Lewis, *Great Divorce*, 85–86.
5. See Lewis, *Screwtape Letters*, 71–72.
6. Lewis, *Great Divorce*, 86, 87.
7. Lewis, *Great Divorce*, 87, emphasis added.
8. See *Summa Theologica* I q. 13, a. 11.
9. Owens, *An Elementary Christian Metaphysics*, 118–24. Philosophically, a transcendental is characteristic of a thing *insofar as it exists*. Insofar as a thing

exists, it is ontologically true, good, and (in its own way) beautiful. Evil, then, is a corruption of a thing's existence. For example, Satan is good insofar as he exists. He is evil insofar as he has corrupted his existence, bringing about a disorder in his existence. In this sense, evil is a *lack*, an absence of good that ought to be there. Importantly, evil can only be parasitic upon the good—evil cannot exist in its own right (much like a cavity in a tooth—the decay is the lack of good health in the tooth).

10. And let us not forget—truth has a name, and a face, in Jesus Christ (Jn 14:6).

11. *Confessions* 1.1 at p. 3, 2.1 at p. 33, emphasis added.

12. Augustine describes his own sin as (virtually) an inexplicable choosing of *nothing*: "Enable my heart to tell you now what it was seeking in this action which made me bad *for no reason*, in which there was *no motive* for my malice except malice. The malice was loathsome, and I loved it. I was in love with my own ruin, *in love with decay*: not with the thing for which I was falling into decay but with decay itself" (*Confessions* 2.4 at p. 41, emphasis added). And yet Augustine knows it is not really nothingness, because evil must piggyback upon some good. For example, the sin might have a sense of nothingness to it, but it does not exist without the sinner, the person doing the action. As Augustine struggles to find genuine motives for his sin, one can glean two from his text: (1) the excitement of wrongdoing; and (2) the camaraderie with his peers, since he tells us he would not have done these things all by himself. (See *Confessions* 2.8 at pp. 47–48).

5. Well-Intended Dysfunction

1. Lewis, *Great Divorce*, 89–90; for this story, see 89–95.
2. Lewis, *Great Divorce*, 89–90, emphasis in original.
3. Lewis, *Great Divorce*, 90, 91, emphasis added.
4. Lewis, *Great Divorce*, 92–93.
5. Lewis, *Great Divorce*, 94–95.
6. See Swafford, *Lunatic, Liar, or Lord*, 24–27.
7. Cited in John Paul II, *Veritatis Splendor* (1993), 71, emphasis in original.
8. Lewis, *Great Divorce*, 77–78, emphasis in original.

6. The Death and Resurrection of Love

1. Lewis, *Great Divorce*, 97–115.
2. Lewis, *Great Divorce*, 98, emphasis in original.
3. Lewis, *Great Divorce*, 99.
4. Lewis, *Great Divorce*, 99, emphasis in original.
5. See Jacques Philippe, *Interior Freedom*, trans. Helena Scott (Scepter, 2007), 44–60.
6. Lewis, *Great Divorce*, 99–100, emphasis in original.

7. Lewis, *Great Divorce*, 100, 102, emphasis in original.

8. Lewis, *Great Divorce*, 100, emphasis added.

9. Wojtyła, *Love and Responsibility*, 119, 120. Wojtyła writes, "The great moral power of true love lies precisely in this longing for the happiness of the other person, that is, for his true good" (120).

10. *Confessions* 5.8 at p. 116.

11. Lewis, *Great Divorce*, 100.

12. See Lewis, *Great Divorce*, 106.

13. Lewis, *Great Divorce*, 107.

14. Lewis, *Great Divorce*, 109.

15. Lewis, *Great Divorce*, 109.

16. Lewis, *Great Divorce*, 109.

17. Lewis, *Great Divorce*, 110.

18. *Confessions* 8.11 at p. 221.

19. Lewis, *Great Divorce*, 110.

20. *Confessions* 8.11 at p. 222, 8.12 at p. 224.

21. C. S. Lewis, *The Voyage of the Dawn Treader* (Scholastic, 1987), 83: "It was, however, clear to everyone that Eustace's character had been rather improved by becoming a dragon."

22. Lewis, *Voyage of the Dawn Treader*, 90, where Eustace describes this momentous event: "The very first tear he made was so deep that I thought it had gone right into my heart. And when he began pulling the skin off, it hurt worse than anything I've ever felt. The only thing that made me able to bear it was just the pleasure of feeling the stuff peel off. You know—if you've ever picked the scab of a sore place. It hurts like billy-oh but *is* such fun to see it coming away" (emphasis in original).

23. Lewis, *Great Divorce*, 111.

24. Lewis, *Great Divorce*, 111, emphasis added.

25. Lewis, *Great Divorce*, 112.

26. See *ST* I q. 1, a. 8, and Andrew Dean Swafford, *Nature and Grace: A New Approach to Thomistic Ressourcement* (Pickwick, 2014), 88–114.

27. Swafford, *Nature and Grace*, 88–100.

28. See Swafford, *Nature and Grace*, 92.

29. Traditionally, reason can know that God exists, as cause of the created effects we see. But reason cannot know the essence of this Uncaused Cause. Reason can only know what God is *not*, by denying of him attributes only properly said of creatures (e.g., creatures are finite, temporal, and changeable, so the Uncaused Cause must be infinite, eternal, and unchangeable).

30. Lewis, *Great Divorce*, 114.

31. Lewis, *Great Divorce*, 114, emphasis in original.

32. Lewis, *Great Divorce*, 114.

33. Lewis, *Great Divorce*, 101.

34. Lewis, *Great Divorce*, 115.

35. Lewis, *Great Divorce*, 106.

36. Karol Wojtyła, *The Jeweler's Shop*, trans. Boleslaw Taborski (Ignatius, 1992), 47–48, 52, 57–61.

37. Wojtyła, *Jeweler's Shop*, 63.

38. Wojtyła, *Jeweler's Shop*, 64 (emphasis added), 65.

39. Wojtyła, *Jeweler's Shop*, 66, emphasis added.

40. Wojtyła, *Jeweler's Shop*, 87, 88–89, emphasis added.

7. Needy Love and Gift Love

1. Lewis, *Great Divorce*, 118, emphasis added.

2. Lewis, *Great Divorce*, 120.

3. See Lewis, *Great Divorce*, 123: "I realized then that they were one person, or rather that both were the remains of what had once been a person."

4. Lewis, *Great Divorce*, 125, emphasis in original.

5. Lewis, *Great Divorce*, 125, emphasis added.

6. Lewis, *Great Divorce*, 126, emphasis in original.

7. Lewis, *Great Divorce*, 126, emphasis in original.

8. Lewis, *Great Divorce*, 127, 130.

9. Lewis, *Great Divorce*, 133.

10. Wojtyła, *Love and Responsibility*, 64, 65.

11. Wojtyła, *Love and Responsibility*, 67.

12. Wojtyła, *Love and Responsibility*, 67.

13. Wojtyła, *Love and Responsibility*, 66.

14. Wojtyła, *Love and Responsibility*, 67–72.

15. See *Aristotle: Nicomachean Ethics*, 8.3 at pp. 121–23.

16. Wojtyła, *Love and Responsibility*, 70, 23, 22, 71.

17. Wojtyła, *Love and Responsibility*, 121.

18. Wojtyła, *Love and Responsibility*, 95, emphasis added.

19. Wojtyła, *Love and Responsibility*, 147, emphasis added.

8. What Is Heaven Like?

1. See Lewis, *Great Divorce*, 1, 69, 112, 9–10.

2. Lewis, *Great Divorce*, 21, emphasis added.

3. Lewis, *Great Divorce*, 24, 65, 23.

4. Lewis, *Great Divorce*, 48, 49, emphasis added.

5. Lewis, *Great Divorce*, 137, 138, emphasis in original.

6. Lewis, *Great Divorce*, 138.

7. Lewis, *Great Divorce*, 138, 139, emphasis in original.

8. See Lewis, *Great Divorce*, 35, 68.

9. The exile also foreshadows the Cross of Jesus, and the community that returns from exile points to both the Resurrection and the Church, as the purified people of God (see *CCC* 710).

10. Lewis, *Great Divorce*, 69.

11. Lewis, *Great Divorce*, 70, emphasis added.

12. Lewis, *Great Divorce*, 70, 71, emphasis added.

13. Lewis, *Great Divorce*, 75, emphasis in original.

14. Hell is the ultimate safeguard of our freedom: "This state of definitive self-exclusion from communion with God and the blessed is called 'hell'" (1033). The time for choosing is now, for upon death, our posture toward or against God becomes fixed, as we enter the realm beyond time and change (see Hebrews 9:27).

15. Penance, indulgences, and purgatory all concern the *temporal* consequences of sin. They have nothing to do with the eternal consequences of sin (see *CCC* 1471).

16. Lewis, *Screwtape Letters*, 174, emphasis in original.

17. The time element stems from lengthy penances done on earth at earlier times in the Church's history. Since there is an organic connection between penance done here and purgatory, the time element (e.g., "five hundred days" off purgatory) was a natural application and extension of the penance done on earth. The Church no longer speaks with such temporal references to purgatory because we have no idea how time functions there. There is clearly a change, a before and after the transformation, so there is a hint of time. But there is no reason to think that our categories of time transfer identically there.

18. D'Ambrosio and Swafford, *What We Believe*, 194.

19. D'Ambrosio and Swafford, *What We Believe*, 195.

20. Lewis, *Mere Christianity*, 136–37.

9. Time and Eternity

1. Lewis, *Great Divorce*, 139–40.

2. Lewis, *Great Divorce*, 139–40, emphasis added. See 1 Peter 3:18–19 and *CCC* 632, as well as *CCC* 634: "The descent into hell brings the Gospel message of salvation to complete fulfillment. This is the last phase of Jesus' messianic mission, a phase which is condensed in time but vast in its real significance: the spread of Christ's redemptive work to all men of all times and all places, for all who are saved have been made sharers in the redemption."

3. Lewis, *Great Divorce*, 140–41.

4. *ST* I q. 10, a. 2.

5. I'm drawing from Jordan Peterson, who likes to define "adventure" as something *one does not know the ending to*—which is precisely why it's risky.

6. We are not lifeless characters in a book, but characters animated with freedom and rationality—perhaps something like actors in a play, with God as the director (though all analogies, of course, break down at some point). And yet, to follow the book analogy, isn't it the case that as an author creates

and develops a given character, such a character often takes a life of its own, as it were, especially as the story develops?

7. "In the earthly liturgy we share in a foretaste of that heavenly liturgy which is celebrated in the Holy City of Jerusalem toward which we journey as pilgrims, where Christ is sitting at the right hand of God, Minister of the sanctuary and of the true tabernacle" (*CCC* 1090, citing *Sacrosanctum Concilium* 8).

8. Of course, this is not to say that the past didn't happen.

9. Lewis, *Screwtape Letters*, 76.

10. See Lewis, *Screwtape Letters*, 112–13.

11. Cited in George Weigel, *Witness to Hope: The Biography of Pope John Paul II* (Cliff Street, 199), 102, emphasis in original.

12. Wojtyła, *Jeweler's Shop*, 64.

13. Wojtyła, *Jeweler's Shop*, 66, emphasis added.

14. See the *Rule of St. Benedict*, ch. 72: "Let them prefer nothing whatever to Christ." Cited in *The Rule of St. Benedict in English*, ed. Timothy Fry (Liturgical Press, 1981), 108–9.

15. Lewis, *Great Divorce*, 109, emphasis added.

10. The Way of Death and the Way of Life

1. Jesus continues to draw on the imagery of trees, both good and bad: "You will know them by their fruits. . . . So, every sound tree bears good fruit, but the bad tree bears evil fruit. A sound tree cannot bear evil fruit, nor can a bad tree bear good fruit" (Mt 7:16–18). See Brant Pitre, *Introduction to the Spiritual Life: Walking the Path of Prayer with Jesus* (Image, 2021), 198–204.

2. Pitre, *Introduction to the Spiritual Life*, 206–7.

3. Wojtła, *Love and Responsibility*, 176, emphasis added.

4. Wojtła, *Love and Responsibility*, 155, 154.

5. Lewis, *Screwtape Letters*, 87.

6. Lewis, *Screwtape Letters*, 88–89. With regard to alcohol, it is not inherently problematic and can certainly enhance the merriment of a social gathering. But drunkenness is a grave sin—one, according to St. Paul, that can exclude us from the kingdom of God (see Galatians 5:21). To get drunk intentionally is to mock two of God's greatest gifts, our intellect and will.

7. In the classical philosophical tradition, enjoying, for example, a sunset is not something we can be intemperate about, owing to its more intellectual and contemplative dimension. See bk. X in *Aristotle: Nicomachean Ethics*, 159–61.

8. Lewis, *Mere Christianity*, 79.

9. See *ST* II–IIae q. 35, a. 1.

10. See Andrew Dean Swafford, *John Paul II to Aristotle and Back Again* (Wipf and Stock, 2015), 43–44.

11. *Confessions* 3.1 at p. 50.

12. *ST* II–IIae q. 127, a. 1 and q. 129, a. 5.
13. *ST* II–IIae q. 36, a. 1.
14. See *ST* II–IIae q. 36, a. 2 and ad 3.
15. See D'Ambrosio and Swafford, *What We Believe*, 185.
16. Lewis, *Screwtape Letters*, 70.
17. Lewis, *Screwtape Letters*, 73.
18. See Swafford, *John Paul II to Aristotle and Back Again*, 44.
19. See Pitre, *Introduction to the Spiritual Life*, 118.
20. See John Paul II, *Centesimus Annus* (1991), nos. 32, 35.
21. See *CCC* 2402–2403 and *ST* II–IIae q. 32, a. 5 ad 2: "The temporal goods which God grants us are ours as to the *ownership*, but as to the *use* of them, they belong not to us alone but also to such others as we are able to succor out of what we have over and above our needs" (emphasis added). See also *ST* II–IIae q. 66, a. 7.
22. So, stealing, for example, is defined as "usurping another's property against the *reasonable* will of the owner" (*CCC* 2408, emphasis added). However, in a state of dire emergency, it would not be considered stealing to utilize another's property to ensure survival, say, with regard to food or shelter (*CCC* 2408).
23. See Lewis, *Screwtape Letters*, 111–15.
24. See Pitre, *Introduction to the Spiritual Life*, 185–94.
25. Pitre, *Introduction to the Spiritual Life*, 192.
26. *Institutes*, 9.13, cited in Pitre, *Introduction to the Spiritual Life*, 193.
27. Adapted from Pitre, *Introduction to the Spiritual Life*, 206–7.
28. Swafford, *Lunatic, Liar, or Lord*, 20.
29. Lewis, *Great Divorce*, 69.
30. 15th World Youth Day Address of the Holy Father John Paul II, Vigil of Prayer, August 19, 2000, no. 5, https://www.vatican.va/content/john-paul-ii/en/speeches/2000/jul-sep/documents/hf_jp-ii_spe_20000819_gmg-veglia.html.
31. See C. S. Lewis, *The Chronicles of Narnia: The Last Battle* (Scholastica, 1988), 161–84.

11. Preparing for the Bridegroom

1. See George Weigel, *The End and the Beginning: Pope John Paul II—The Victory of Freedom, the Last Years, the Legacy* (Image, 2010), 24–27.
2. Cited in Jack Fairweather, *The Volunteer: The True Story of the Resistance Hero Who Infiltrated Auschwitz* (Custom House, 2019), 384.
3. "There is no surer pledge or clearer sign of this great hope in the new heavens and new earth 'in which righteousness dwells' [2 Pt 3:13] than the Eucharist. Every time this mystery is celebrated, 'the work of our redemption is carried on' and we 'break the one bread that provides the medicine of

immortality, the antidote for death, and the food that makes us live for ever in Jesus Christ'" [Ignatius of Antioch, AD 107] (*CCC* 1405).

4. It is fitting that we reflect on such texts in light of Christ's coming at the end of time (as we often do during Advent), because just as the Temple in its biblical symbolism embodies creation, so the fall of the Temple prefigures the end of all things.

5. In Greek, *ousia* means "being," and *para* means "alongside."

6. Wojtyła, *Jeweler's Shop*, 62–63.

7. "Death puts an end to human life as the time open to either accepting or rejecting the divine grace manifested in Christ" (*CCC* 1021). This is called the "particular judgment."

8. This is the called the "Last" or "General Judgment" (see *CCC* 1038–1041).

9. Lewis, *Great Divorce*, 75.

10. Lewis, *Great Divorce*, 109.

Andrew Swafford is a professor of theology at Benedictine College. He is the author of *Lunatic, Liar, or Lord: Unveiling the Truth of Catholicism with C. S. Lewis's Mere Christianity* and *A Catholic Guide to the New Testament*. Together with his wife, Sarah Swafford, he coauthored *Gift and Grit: How Heroic Virtue Can Change Your Life and Relationships*.

Swafford holds a doctor of sacred theology degree from the University of St. Mary of the Lake and a master's degree in Old Testament and Semitic languages from Trinity Evangelical Divinity School. He has spoken at numerous conferences, including the National Catholic Youth Conference (NCYC), the National Eucharistic Congress, the RENEW Toronto conference for young adults, and the Defending the Faith Conference in Steubenville, Ohio. He has also been featured on Fox News and Chris Cuomo's *News Nation*.

Swafford is the general editor of and a contributor to Ascension's *Great Adventure Catholic Bible*. An avid student of Brazilian jiu-jitsu, he lives in Atchison, Kansas, with Sarah and their children.

theswaffords.com
X: @andrew_swafford